Between the Gas Works and the Church

By
Mike Axworthy

First published 2011 by Countyvise Ltd
14 Appin Road, Birkenhead, CH41 9HH

British Library Cataloguing in Publication Data.
A catalogue record for this book is available from the British Library.

ISBN 978 1 906823 48 1

Dedication

This book is dedicated to
Patrick McCarthy Axworthy (Dad)
Marjorie Axworthy (Nee Yates Jones) (Mum)
and my family.

Introduction

Since finishing work through ill health, I have had a long time to think and many times have thought I would like to record childhood memories and put them onto paper before I forget them. Well I have decided at last to put pen to paper. The catalyst was as a result of reading a book by the actor Dirk Bogarde in which he gave advice to a friend who was ill, and consequently had time on her hands to write her memoirs. I thought this was good advice, so I took the challenge up myself.

I have written two versions of these memories, one in prose, and the other in blank verse. The words are illustrated with many pictures, hoping to bring the story to life. My story is a personal history, bringing echoes from the past to the present. I think you will find it is a common history of many of us from that era. I hope you enjoy the memories of childhood, I certainly enjoyed writing them.

Liverpool Born Garston Bred

Memories Of A Garston Childhood In The 1950s

There is only one thing better than a Liverpool childhood, that's a Garston childhood. I was born in Liverpool in 1950 a great seaport and city and back then it was still a major trading and manufacturing city. The River Mersey, the major artery of the city, with its tide rushing in twice a day, bringing with it the great liners that crossed the Atlantic to and from America, this before the airlines expanded during the Sixties and Seventies killing off this trade. Also cargo vessels from all points of the earth brought in millions of tons of imports and took out the same amount in exports. The river also had tugboats, pleasure craft, dredgers, fishing boats and the famous ferryboats, which in those days sailed regularly between Liverpool and Birkenhead, Wallasey and New Brighton.

Above: Garston with Liverpool in the distance.

Above: The Gas Tank and Garston Parish Church.

The docks stretched between Crosby in the North to Garston in the South. Garston would play a major part in my life in later years, more of that later. The docks had such famous names as Canada, Langton, Clarence, Huskinson, Waterloo, and The Albert Docks and many more. The river at the Pierhead was fronted by probably three of the most famous and magnificent buildings in the world, They were the Liver Buildings, the Cunard Buildings and the Mersey Docks and Harbour Company's building. Into this Pool of Life I was born in the Oxford Street hospital on 7th November 1950 - mother and baby both well after the birth.

My mother was Marjorie Yates Jones and my father was Patrick McCarthy Axworthy. I was not their first born as in January of that same year Mother had given birth to a son, Francis, who in circumstances of great sadness died three days after the birth without my Mother holding the baby, so cruel and insensitive were the hospitals in those days. But the one thing they did take note of was the Doctor, again, probably a bit hard, who told them to try again for another baby as soon as possible, this they did and I arrived 10 months later.

After six days confinement, mother and baby were allowed home, I was a bouncing 8lb baby. Home then was a top floor flat in Wellfield Place in Dingle. The Dingle was a very vibrant place centred mainly on Park Road, a thriving shopping and trading area stretching from the ancient Toxteth Chapel at the south end of Park Road, to St Patrick's Catholic Church at the north end. In between were hundreds of shops, a pub on every corner, churches, and a cinema opposite the chapel. Wellfield Place was at the South end of Park Road just off Peel Street. The house itself was a grand old three-storey house originally belonging to the wealthy merchant classes who sprang up during the boom time in the development of Liverpool as a major trading and business centre, second only to London at that time.

My father's mother, Bridget McCarthy Axworthy had bought the house as a family investment and at the time that we lived there my parents and two of my father's brothers Ernie and Frank also lived there.

I would not be surprised if my mother wished she had stayed in Garston where she had lived all her life. She would one day have her hopes fulfilled, and return back home, but more of that later.

Welsh English Mother

Marjorie Yates Jones, to give my Mum her full maiden name, was born and bred at 20 Ultonia Street, Garston. She was born upstairs, in the little terraced house, that was part of a block of streets all called after ships of the White Star Shipping Line, including Campania, Lucania, Umbria, and of course also part of the fleet was the great 'unsinkable ship', 'The Titanic' which hit an iceberg on its maiden voyage. The names of the streets were very grand but unfortunately the houses were not, two up and two down, and an outside water tap and lavatory. You had to take a bath in front of the black range with its blazing fire, oven for cooking and the kettle was always on the go on top of the range. The House had been brand spanking new when my Gran moved in and she was always very proud of it. I always admired the brickwork, which was a change from the usual terraced houses of 'under the bridge'. They were built of a lovely yellow brick at the top with red brick at the bottom and the usual grey Welsh slate roof. The Welsh slate was very appropriate as the Welsh built a lot of Garston. Up the Village, as St Mary's Road was known, on one of its buildings there is a lovely carved sandstone with the motto 'Ich Dien' (I serve) and the 3 plumes of the Prince of Wales' badge.

Above: Marjorie Yates Jones.

My mother, herself, as the name Yates Jones suggests, had Welsh blood. Her 'ninny' or grandmother always spoke Welsh and never learned to speak English. So like many people living 'under the bridge', Marjorie had a mixed background of English and Welsh. My mother was blonde, blue eyed and beautiful. The rest of my Mum's family were: her half sister Doris, who was the eldest child; half brothers Freddy and Sammy and sister Olive who was the youngest. The unusual thing about this was that the half brothers and sisters were also named Jones's as their fathers were both Jones and Emily married Frank Yates Jones after her first husband Samuel Jones had died.

Scottish Irish Dad

My father had an altogether more difficult start to life. For reasons not completely known my father was born in Largs in Scotland in a hotel and not long after that he was taken to Ireland and

Above: Patrick McCarthy Axworthy.

brought up there. His father Aaron Malcolm Axworthy was a bit of a roamer and left his wife Bridie a few times but kept periodically turning up again. It was during these difficult times that father was conceived.

When Patrick was due to be born his Dad had gone missing again, and his mother, who had been working as a teacher, had to keep him secret hence the trip out of town for the birth. At that time she would have had to give up her job if she had a baby at home.

For the rest of his life my father would nostalgically talk about the magic of a childhood spent on an Irish farm, very poor, harsh at times but very peaceful and healthy, never to be forgotten. After many years of Irish life, having known nothing else, his mother turned up in Ireland to take him to England. This shocked and terrified my Dad, who tried and succeeded in escaping from the train and got out the other side of the carriage and ran for his life. He was caught and given a good hiding from his mother. This was the first of many and he wished many times to be back in Ireland.

To be brought to Liverpool, a noisy, vibrant and large city from a farm in Ireland was a great shock. He had even more of a shock when he discovered he had five brothers and one sister, they were in order of age, Ernie, Jimmy, Frank, Billy, Euphemia, and the baby of the family Ian.

The Axworthy family now lived in a very large Victorian house in Wellfield Place in the Dingle as I related earlier and this was the home to which I was brought to after my birth many years later.

Patrick McCarthy Axworthy had to attend school, which was difficult for him, as he had missed a couple of years schooling, and also had a slight Irish accent. The school he attended was Mount Carmel Catholic School in High Park Street. His one abiding memory of the school was winning a prize – a marmalade dish in a school gala.

Evacuation and War

My mother, Marjorie, attended Banks Road County Primary School; had no great academic record, but her one surviving school report states that she was well behaved and very neat and tidy.

Above: School children Evacuated from Garston.

As all children of that day the war came to wreak havoc on any remaining schooldays for both Mum and Dad. My mum was evacuated to Llangollen in Wales. She vividly remembers being lined up with other children as the prospective new carers chose their new lodgers.

My mother was chosen by a doctor and his wife but there was a problem, Olive, my mum's sister screamed until the doctor agreed to take her as well and mum was under orders from home to look after her and would not let go of her hand until they both had the same home.

This time in Wales was very happy for my mother. It was a beautiful part of the world on a river with lovely views but also the doctor's family were very kind and caring about the girls' welfare.

This idyllic time was brought to an end when my mum's parents wanted the girls to go back home. The ferocious blitz on Liverpool of the early part of the war had died down and mum's parents felt that it would be safe for them to return home.

The Blitz

Liverpool had taken a terrific pounding from the air. Many buildings were razed to the ground and thousands of people died. It was obviously a target because of its strategic importance as a major port and the centre of the Western Approaches operations.

Garston reflected this position as a port and manufacturing centre. Many bombs aimed for the docks missed and hit nearby streets, flattening houses and killing civilians. The risk was not completely over when my mum returned home as was proved when a land mine came down in the gas tank, which dominated the skyline of Garston. Luckily it did not explode and was safely defused by Captain Newgas. This event became part of local history and was spoken of as the time Garston nearly blew up. The population of Under the Bridge were evacuated out of the area for safety, later that night fuelled by drink, mum's father decided to go back home in Ultonia Street. He took hold of my mum's hand and marched up to the barrier stopping you from going back under the bridge, he went to go through but the police stopped him, after a bit of an argument they sent him and my mum back to his mother-in-law's in Wellington Street. I think my mother was very relieved and her dad got a telling off from the family.

Right: The gas tank Arial - from which a land mine was defused.

Dad's War

My father's experience of the war was very different. At the beginning of the conflict he was only fourteen, too young to join up. He was also evacuated and once again his mother sent him and his younger brother Ian to the family farm in Ireland. My father spoke of this time on the farm as very happy days in his life. He told us stories of farm life: riding the donkey and trap, spading the turf, bringing in the hay, milking the cows, feeding the hens, and fishing in the river Feale which ran at the bottom of the fields.

Above: Father home from the War (centre).

After a few years of bliss in Ireland his mother took ill, so dad came back to Liverpool; sadly his Mother died. After his mother died, dad now nearly eighteen, had to make up his mind should he go back to the farm or should he join up, he decided to join up. So in 1944 dad joined the Royal Engineers (REME) and he loved every minute of it. He excelled and was named recruit of the year and even represented his regiment at boxing at which he was very adept. He also saw service in, France, Germany, Norway, and finally Palestine.

Like so many other soldiers on leaving the Army, dad drifted from job to job, and that wasn't difficult as there were plenty of jobs to be had. Still being a young man he had a very active social life, this consisted of, going for a pint or two in the many pubs around town, or going to the pictures in the local cinema, or his favourite pastime, dancing in the Rialto in Parliament Street.

War Over

At the other end of the city, in Garston, my mum had finished her schooling, and now looked for a job. Like all working class girls of that era she finished school at fourteen and went straight into the labour market. There were plenty of jobs to be had and the biggest employer in Garston at that time was the Bobbin Works who employed thousands of people. The Bobbins were made of wood and the logs came down the river, off loaded onto rail tracks at Garston Docks and then took the short journey to the Bobbin Works. The timber would then be made into millions of bobbins and shuttles at the largest bobbin maker in the world at that time. It was very hard work and there were plenty of accidents.

It was also hard at home when she had to do her share of the chores. This included cleaning, ironing, washing and cooking. Everything relied on the black range, heating, hot water, cooking and even the flat iron was warmed on the top of the range.

Though they were hard, they were happy days, especially as it was not long since the war ended and people were glad to be at peace even if rationing was still in existence.

In Umbria Street the pleasures were simple but fun. Emily, my Gran, liked a little drink and was quite talented on the piano and the two went together when she played the ivories in the Canterbury Hotel. No doubt Frank, my Granddad, was in the crowd being entertained. He also like a drink or two and possibly rolled home a few times.

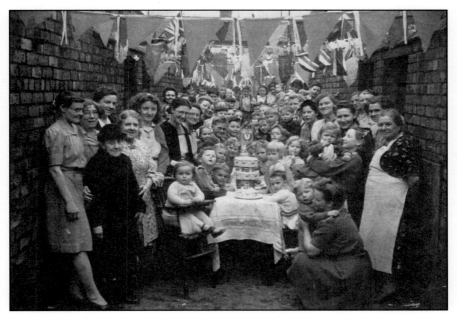

Above: Ultonia Street VE day street Party.

Time To Dance

My Mum grew into a beautiful woman as old photographs show, people's comments will also testify. Mum also became a very accomplished dancer and loved to go out with her friends to the many dance halls in Liverpool.

At Garston baths, boards were put over the pool at the weekend and so it became the local dance hall. One dubious nickname was the 'blood baths' because of the frequent fights between the local toughs and the 'peanut gang' from the Dingle.

One night Mum and some friends decided to go to the Rialto in Parliament Street, then a very smart dance hall that served not only tea and coffee but a very genteel atmosphere. As my Mother and her friend danced she noticed a very smart and handsome dark haired man coming across the dance floor. He stopped in front of her, as was the norm and asked her formally for a dance. "No" she said. Father went back to his chair crestfallen but not bowed and as he would show many times in his life, he did not give up easily. He tried a second time later on that night and this time he was successful. After the dance he made a date to meet Marjorie again. This began the courtship that would eventually lead to marriage.

Wedding Bells

They got married in Mount Carmel church in the Dingle. As it was October, it was a cold day but the bride and groom both looked resplendent in their best, Father in a dark blue, double breasted suit and Mother in a radiant turquoise suit.

They took their vows and went outside for the obligatory photographs. This is where one of the most disappointing moments in Mum's life took place. She wouldn't know for a week but the photographs did not turn out. Uncle Ian, dad's brother was in charge of recording the great day and he had put the film in wrong and that spelt disaster. Unlike modern times when every major event is saturated with cameras and video cameras, a camera was a luxury and difficult to use, hence the total sadness of not being recorded for posterity. To add to the irony Mum's parents said to her that there was a portrait photographer in Park Road only 50 yards away. They said for her to go and get her portrait done with her new husband but this offer was turned down not realising the disaster that was unfolding.

Above: Mum and Dad and me at Wellfield Place.

The wedding breakfast was held at Wellfield Place, a large Victorian 3 storey dwelling left to the Axworthy Brothers by their Mother on her death. Patrick had one room on the top floor and this is where the newly wedded couple would start their married life. This was not a perfect start in life but it was a lot better than most. To have your own room, a bathroom and toilet on the landing was considered luxurious.

A big problem arose when I was born in the November of 1950, as we lived on the top floor and there were a lot of stairs to get up with a pram. An opportunity arose that gave them a chance to get out of this situation. Frank offered the keys to his prefab in exchange for £30. My parents accepted this offer even though it was not strictly legal.

Prefab Country

The prefab was situated in Gateacre which at that time was out in the country on the edge of Liverpool. At the end of the war there was a need for new housing to replace the property that had been blitzed during the bombing. As there were still economic difficulties after the war, they came up with the idea of cheap prefabricated single storey property. They might have been cheap but they were very popular, and as most of the tenants came from poor housing they found the prefabs surprisingly nice. They were modern, had hot water, bathrooms, indoor toilets, and a nice garden. The one criticism made of the prefabs over the years was they were extremely cold in the Winter, this was due to the material they were made of.

Above: Prefab in Bellvale.

The family moved in – now consisting of another member Patrick Jnr born 1st of May 1952, this was another reason to leave Wellfield Place, more room was needed. The move to leafy Gateacre seemed an opportunity for a new start. Although Mum liked the Prefab, she felt a bit lonely, longing for the security and warmth she felt in her old home of Garston. Her family and all her old friends still lived in Garston and she longed to be there among the comforting noise, smells, and the hustle and bustle of a thriving dockside community.

My father didn't feel too happy about this, as he felt settled, and quite liked the semi-rural life of Gateacre. Once again he would have to uproot, something he had done many times in his life. He could not see what Garston offered a young family! He only saw, gas holders, factories, streets cheek to jowl with each other, pubs on every corner, and when he went – under the bridge – he felt like a fish out of water.

Going Back Home

My mum would not give in, and when she was offered the chance to exchange her prefab for a terraced house in Derby Street, she pleaded with dad to accept, saying she would be Happy ever after. Finally dad relented though with some reservations, but how could he turn down such a lament. Soon we were on our way to our new home in Garston and would live there until the house was demolished thirty years later. The house 30 Derby Street was a traditional terrace house built at the end of the 19th century.

After living in the cosy prefab with its bathroom and hot water, Derby Street was a bit basic. It was a solidly built house of local made brick (a lot of the houses in this area were built from local brick made in the brickfields of Garston) it had three bedrooms but no bathroom or hot water, and the toilet was at the bottom of the yard. This was no problem to my mum, who was thrilled to be back in the community she had grown up in, the streets of "Under the Bridge."

*Above: Clifton Street on the right, where Mum's
Dad grew up.*

The area was flanked on one side by the docks and river, and
on the other side by Industry and the Gasworks, and alongside
the river the airport. The main entrance to this community was
by Church Road which ran under the railway bridge, hence the
name given to this area. If you lived here many thought you
lived on the wrong side of the tracks, but if you did live here
many people would not want to live anywhere else.

Under The Bridge

If you were to design the perfect community then Garston had
to be added to it, surrounded by industry and the docks there
was plenty of work to be had. Everything you needed to buy
was available locally, most streets had the mandatory corner
shop, or there was Window Lane with its many shops, and if
that wasn't enough there were the Garston Village shops. The
social life was well catered for, there were many pubs – too

many to list – there were social clubs for every taste – church clubs, working men's clubs, snooker clubs, football clubs, buffalo clubs, Masonic clubs, there were well over forty pubs and clubs in this small place called Garston. There were schools for those with religious affiliations and schools for those without any affiliation, and for every denomination there were Church or Chapel or Mission hall, even a Mission hall for the sailors that sailed into Garston Docks, so spiritual food was available to everyone.

For the children there were parks with swings, slides, monkey ladders, merry go rounds, and maypoles; for the adults there were bowling greens and benches to sit on and admire the trees and flowers of the parks. There were fields to walk your dog or to play football or cricket on, there were libraries to educate and entertain the mind, and in walking distance there were the woods of Woolton and Speke Hall, the meadows and fields of Allerton, and we could also walk up the shore, with its river, its ponds and fields.

Growing Family

I was four years old when I moved into our new home in Garston, the memories are vague but some events I do remember. It wasn't long after we moved in when a new addition was added to the family. I never noticed my mother was having a baby nor do I remember the birth, but have been told since of my dad's attempt at stopping the birth. Timothy came in a rush before the midwife arrived, so dad in a futile attempt at stopping the birth pushed hard down on my mum's head hoping this would stop the birth. He was unsuccessful and Tim was born in a hurry and made his entry on the living room floor. Mother and baby were both fine, and when the midwife arrived all she had to do was cut the cord and weigh the baby.

Starting School

It was about this time I started school, I would go to Holy Trinity catholic school on Banks Road only a few hundred yards from our house. My mother took me on my first day; this was the only day she took me. I liked going on my own and I wasn't a bit nervous, I enjoyed school and made friends easily. I remember the classroom had what seemed like a giant doll's house in the corner; we played and pushed each other to get inside. In the morning the register was called, I answered with pride, and then we said prayers.

Above: Holy Trinity School.

Christmas was fun, we made decorations and painted snow scenes, then we made angels for the Christmas tree. The teacher held a raffle and I won it – a chocolate log – I took it home, we all tucked in, enjoyed the taste and I smiled.

It didn't seem long before the year ended and I left the infants class, and started in the junior class.

They were carefree days and I enjoyed them, I liked school and made friends easily, but still liked going home to play in the street. This was the era of making your own fun and as soon as school ended we were out in the street, or off to the park. Home for us was where we got fed and went to bed, not to sit in and do homework.

Home Entertainment

In the house we still had no television, we did have a piano, a guitar, and an accordion. These all belonged to dad, he played all of them a bit, but mastered none. What he could do was sing, dad had a good tenor voice, sounding like Joseph Locke the great Irish tenor. Even when in the street we could hear dad singing, he sang all kinds of songs but mostly ballads. Because we had no artificial entertainment, we made our own fun, often we joined in the singing and this for me this was the beginning of a lifetime love of music. The music at home was more fun than the music at school which consisted of a piano and out of tune hymns. I remember my maternal Grandmother visiting us and playing the piano, we all joined in the singing, gran said it was just like the Canterbury pub where she played.

My favourite music was rousing sing alongs. As well as these dad sang a lot of Irish ballads and also Bing Crosby songs. The front room were all the musical instruments were, we called the parlour. We had to ask permission to go in the posh room, but I often sneaked in for a strum on the guitar or a squeeze of the accordion, or a play of the piano. My dad always found out, especially if I broke a string on the guitar, or left mucky fingers on the keys of the accordion or piano. We were lucky – our next door neighbours liked the music; they could easily have complained. My mum said to them once she was sorry about the noise and music. The neighbours just said don't worry we enjoy it, and we feel safer with your family next door. In fact the lady next door used to pass bananas over the wall for us, her son worked on the Garston Docks, so we always knew when a banana boat was in, I loved the bananas! especially on a butty.

Healthy Eating

I always enjoyed my food, and ate whatever was put in front of me – you had no choice – eat it or go hungry. The food was basic but wholesome, and bought from the local shops on the day. Breakfast never changed, it was always porridge oats with milk and sugar. The only variation was sometimes it was thick and lumpy, other times thin and runny. Luckily I liked it and as mum said it put a lining on your stomach for the day. Lunch was just a snack, jam butties with tea, dinner or tea as we called it was the main meal of the day, always a hot cooked meal, whatever it was I ate it, and even licked the plate, no waste in our house. Before bed we had supper, a piece of toast, unless you had been naughty, then you went without.

Above: Banana Boat in Garston Dock.

It must have been a healthy diet as we were all fit and didn't bother the doctor much, and we soon burned off any excess as we were never still. At this time I was very slim, blond as a Viking, and as brown as a berry. It was at this age of 7 or 8 I started to play football. I soon became fanatical, the ball was never far away from my feet. I kicked a ball on the way to school, in the school playground, and then after school. A bigger lad in the street – Micky O'Neill – was a wizard with the ball, and he taught me many tricks and juggling skills and how to dribble. It turned out Micky was also a great cricketer and played for Liverpool cricket team, he tried to teach me the arts of cricket as well, but I was never as good at cricket.

Playing With Fire

As children we were always warned about the danger of fire, and unfortunately many children ignore the refrain 'Do not play with fire'. My brother and I did and nearly paid the price.

Above: Now we are three, Tim still looking shocked from the fire (centre).

My mother decided to clean the front step, when she did she always ended up chatting to a neighbour or people passing by, but before she went out she told us to watch the toddler 'Tim' and he lay sleeping strapped in his pram. We did this then felt bored, we noticed matches on the fireplace, so decided to light a fire. We found an old newspaper and started to experiment, we put the shovel on the fireplace, like father did, we placed a sheet of newspaper across the shovel then lit it. The paper turned brown then burst into flames, paper flew everywhere, we chased the burning paper trying to put the flames out, but one piece we missed and soon the settee caught fire, smoke was everywhere. What a scene, we heard the baby cry, we ran out of the house screaming for mum, she rushed past us, in seconds she was back with the pram, then rushed in again with the bucket of water, luckily she put the fire out, but the setee was ruined. My brother and I got a scolding, and then heard those dreaded words 'wait till your father comes home'. We got a smacking and sent to bed with no supper. That was the last time I played with fire.

Laughter And Tears

When you are a child you just accept what comes along, another baby, dad losing his job, mum becoming ill, no food in the cupboard, whatever it was we just got on with it. I thought every family's life was like this, and to an extent it was. Our family had to be resilient, and no problem would keep us down for long, there was always laughter after tears, life was just one big adventure.

This was as true of school as it was of home. This is where you got over disappointments, learned about discipline, how to make friends and avoid the bullies. I grew up fast and was quite astute, keeping well in with most people, and I wasn't a soft touch. If I was attacked I could well defend myself, dad had made sure of that, with boxing lessons, and using sayings, like bullies are cowards, stand up to them and they think twice before they bully you again. This was true of the street as well, but mostly we all got on well in the street, we all played together; there was always something to do, and places to go. In the summers we were never in, except when we were hungry or thirsty, and then a jam butty was lovely, and a cold drink out of the tap was beautiful, the sweetest drink I ever tasted, 'Corpy Pop' we called it.

Sometimes the sun beat down so hot it melted the tar in the street, and we loved to burst the tar bubbles that came up, the problem was, we ended up with tar on our clothes, in our hair, and stuck to our knees.

Tin Bath and Overcoats

When we went in of an evening we were scrubbed. We would be told off about the tar and then would be the scrubbing in the bath. Dad would get a scrubbing brush and scrub until we screamed for mercy. Sometimes he scrubbed so hard to get the tar off, the skin on our knees would redden and peel off.

I liked to be first in the bath because the water was clean; by the time he came to my brothers it was full of scum.

The bath was tin and most of the time hung on a nail in the yard, only being brought in for bath time. The hot water would be boiled on the cooker in pans then brought in the living room, were the bath stood in front of the fireplace. The water would then be poured into the bath. If you stepped in too quick you might get a shock as it was too hot and you would hop about like a scalded cat, until mum brought in cold water to cool the temperature.

One incident I remember with the tin bath was to earn me another good hiding. Patrick and I took it off its perch in the yard to play drums and then for no good reason we decided to see if we could hammer a nail through the tin, in this we succeeded and then we put the bath back.

This deed went unnoticed until bath time, and when the filling was attempted the bath would not fill and the water seeped over the floor. When the hole was discovered the result was inevitable, a good smacking on our bare bottoms, that's if he could catch us. We were like scared rabbits and dodged and squirmed but we always got caught and always got a smack on the leg, arm, bum or face. We didn't cry. We tended to laugh at smacks. Once again this made us tougher and impervious to pain, so to be smacked and to smack was to us the norm.

After being washed we would all sit around the fire, no telly then, and we would entertain ourselves. This would consist of dad telling stories or singing songs in which we all joined in, or dancing around the room. On more boisterous nights, encouraged by dad, we had wrestling and strength competitions. Dad used to balance us on his arms or legs, lifting us into the air. This was great unless he lost his balance and you fell.

Another strength game was to hold the poker and try to pull your opponent up by putting your feet against his and both holding and pulling on the poker. A lot of these games ended in fisticuffs and tears but I think we enjoyed this as well.

Bedtime was always resisted, but even here the war continued, fighting over blankets and coats. As the song says, we did sleep under old coats and my favourite was dad's old full-length army khaki coat and I would battle to keep it. You made sure you took the bucket upstairs, as there was no indoor toilet; the bucket served the purpose if you needed to go in the night. This you tried to do without disturbing the whole house. This might seem primitive but it was not possible to go down to the bottom of the yard in the middle of the night, especially in the winter when it was pitch black and often freezing.

In the winter the outside toilet often froze so a night light candle was put in to stop the cistern freezing, but this did nothing for your bum when you sat down. It was the one place you didn't hang around in the winter.

The school was the same; the toilets were outside in the playground. In the summer, to get out of class, you would put your hand up to ask if you could go to the toilet. This was allowed but if the teacher thought you were abusing this system she would say no. This was fine until one of the boys who had been turned down had an accident in class and caused a terrible stink in more ways than one.

Now We Are Four

We continued to learn, which I enjoyed, but I was distracted by my obsessive love of football. Always looking out of the window at the Match Works field where there where goal posts, dreaming of scoring goals.

One day we were playing football on the park where the teacher had taken us for games. I was trying to impress her with my skills and was thrilled when she commented on this and told me to report to Mr Kelly. I was only eight at the time and Mr Kelly who was a legend, ran the school Under Tens football team and he needed a couple of players.

His team were a year older than I was but it turned out they had reached the semi-final in a competition and were short of a couple of players, due to injury. I was picked for the game that took place at Penny Lane, a ground where Liverpool Boys played and also the place the Beatles would make famous years later in a song.

I remember bits of the occasion even now. We were narrowly beaten but a man named Mr Rylands made a remark to my dad, who also came to watch the match that I was a good player and could go places. This was music to my ears and a great encouragement to go on training and practising.

All too rarely in my view were we given praise in those days as it was seen as a way of making you bigheaded, especially if you did have talent. I could never understand this attitude as encouragement goes a long way to nurture talent. Too much criticism can destroy a brittle self-belief.

Above: Now we are four.

Life at home was still hard but happy, there were four boys but I was very much engrossed in my own interests and myself and didn't take much notice of the younger ones.

Occasionally I would play with Patrick, the brother nearest in age to me, but generally his hobbies were different. He liked birds, catapults, going bird egging and his friends tended to be a bit rougher and got into more trouble in the neighbourhood. If we got into trouble and a visit was paid to the door, mum would chastise us but usually it was "wait until your father gets home". Mum liked to use the brush handle to give us a bash.

Once she made the mistake of hitting me with her bare hand and hitting my hard head, she broke her finger. That night I paid the price, with a double whacking from dad.

A Working Life

Mum had it hard, she never complained and she worked very hard for the family. There were no modern appliances to help with the chores. She washed by hand, scrubbing away on the drainer by the Belfast sink. There always seemed to be nappies soaking or on the line strung across the yard, propped up by a wooden pole. On wet days the washing was hung indoors on a clothes maiden that was lowered and lifted up by a pulley. The clothes maiden was in the living room and it often dripped on those underneath. There was always a damp smell of washing drying, I remember the pulley collapsing once with all the weight and we got a smack on the head. Heavy washing, like sheets, blankets and curtains were taken to the Wash House in Garston village, on a pram. I sometimes tagged along and was fascinated by the hustle and bustle, the noise, the steam hissing and the women jangling.

Preparing meals must have been a strain as well. No way would we ever turn down food, we would eat what was put in front of us; if you left it you went hungry. Food would always be fresh as it was usually bought on the day in the local shops. You could get anything within a couple of hundred yards of our front door. There were the butchers, grocers, fishmongers, dairies, bakers' cake shops, fish and chip shops and sweet shops in Window Lane. We even had our own corner shop, Kettlewells. Mum would send me for a pound of mince or 5lb of spuds, or a loaf, and always said, "Make sure you don't drop the money, and bring back the change". If I was lucky I could spend the change on sweets, like a penny arrow bar, sherbet dips, broken biscuits, chocolate eclairs, love hearts, sticky lice or liquorice. The staple diet was porridge, potatoes and bread and jam. Every day mum had to shop for the food, then prepare it; she was always peeling potatoes; and then finally to cook it. The meals were delicious and tasty, never any left but if there was any left on a plate I would usually finish it off, and then lick the plate clean. Scouse went down well. This was a form of Irish stew but a bit thicker, hence the nickname, "lob" scouse. Mince and potatoes; yellow fish with beans; corned beef; sausage and mash. All plain food, but none the worse for that.

Above: The Bobbin Works, Garston.

Mum did all the washing and cooking as well as cleaning the house, making the beds, getting us ready for school and ironing. As if that wasn't enough, she worked part time in the mirror works and the Bobbin works.

The cleaning was hard, all mop and bucket, brushing up and scrubbing the floors, whitening the step and cleaning the windows. When I think of it we could have done with a maid to help mum, being a mother was not easy, especially with four boys. Father worked hard to provide for his family. There was the odd period of insecurity as he got and lost a few jobs.

Fatherhood was not easy either, having the worry of providing and protecting a growing family.

I don't think he ever quite found his vocation, he had many strengths and skills but never quite put these to the best use, he tended to get fed up and wanted to try something else.

On my birth certificate his occupation is given as handyman and driver in a girls college. The first job I remember was his position as a driver of a lorry for a building firm, but I know before that, he worked in Tate and Lyle sugar makers, Dunlop tyre makers and the Bottle works that made all kinds of glass.

But to us, like most children, dad was big, larger than life, the boss, and protector. He would make everything right, take away your fears, fix anything from a broken window to leaking taps, blocked drains, blown fuses, in fact anything that needed repairing or fixing, he would do it.

Dad was always very independent as far as transport went. He would either have a pushbike or a motorbike, and in later years, a car.

Spreading My Wings

Now that I was eight years of age I started to spread my wings a bit. I loved to roam, to go on long walks and be out in the fresh air.

We were surrounded on all sides by industry and railways, but we were lucky in that not far away there was a lot of open countryside to go playing in.

A place I loved to go was up the shore. This was an area of coastline alongside the River Mersey. The walks were sandwiched between the mud of the river and the airport further on, Speke Hall, and still further, the farmers' fields on to Hale lighthouse.

Above: Garston Hospital, before demolition.

It was a popular place, especially the first field on the walk where Garstonians played and sat and just watched the world go by. One day I recall as a young child of four I was on the field with my parents when I ran away up to some boys who were playing with fire. They had rubber tyres in the fire, and then as they melted they would twirl them around to watch the flaming rubber shoot off. One piece of rubber flew towards me and stuck on the inside of my right arm. The screams were relentless, the pain excruciating and my parents upset and angry with the boys. I was pushed to the hospital, cleaned up and bandaged. I was left with a scar, in the shape of a horseshoe, for the rest of my life.

The local hospital, named "Sir Alfred Lewis Jones" after its benefactor, was on the site of the old fever hospital on the hill of Kettle Nook, looking down on the crossroads of Garston. On opposite corners of the crossroads were the pubs the Queens and the Mona and on the other corner, the grocers Irwins. The hospital also faced the cinema, the Empire. I only went occasionally to the cinema, as the entrance money was prohibitive although I did manage to bunk in a couple of times through the emergency exits.

Flash Gordon was the Saturday hero then and I also remember the Three Stooges and the Lone Ranger. Like all cinemas it was known as the fleapit.

It was not all play. I still had school. For the most part I tried hard in school, but all my school reports say I tended to be distracted too easily and I talked too much. But I did try, I struggled at Maths, did well in English and Religious Studies. I also enjoyed History and Geography. Art I enjoyed but was not fussy on papier-mâché puppet making and we seemed to do that a lot. Mix up papers with glue and then mould this mix into sculptures.

Out of hours school activities interested me more. A great place to go was the Play Centre in Banks Road School, from 5 p.m. until 8 p.m. They had snooker and table tennis tables, five a side football, drawing, painting, a music room and all kinds of skipping ropes, balls and bean bags, a feast of fun and games. This was organised by local teachers, some from our school, but it was far more relaxed than school. The equipment wasn't great but it didn't matter, we just enjoyed ourselves. There was the occasional scrap but nothing too serious and it was a good place to mix as it was non-denominational. Boys and girls came from all local schools, and guess what? - We were all just the same. The same hopes and fears needs and wants. All the boys started to like girls and vice versa, we were all chasing each other once and I ran in the cloakrooms and crashed my head into a coat hook. Blood splattered everywhere. I raced home blood trailing behind. When my mother saw me she nearly died. I was covered in blood, but it looked worse than it was, once I was cleaned up and a couple of stitches put in I was back out playing.

Football Crazy Football Mad

I still excelled at sport and it was about now I started to say I wanted to be a footballer. I was so keen I hardly had a ball out of my sight and practised on the park every evening until it went dark.

Above: Garston boys playing football.

I had my bedroom plastered with pictures of footballers. No need for wallpaper here. I shared this bedroom with Patrick who had no interest in football, but he put up with it. I told anyone who would listen that I would be a footballer and as hundreds of other boys said the same this was just thought of as a boyhood dream. Most boys played football, if you didn't you were thought of as a sissy, not quite right, and those few boys were usually teased unmercifully.

I loved to play with the bigger boys on the park. I was always picked last as I was the smallest and I was known as little Mick. But I already had skill and I was very determined and proved an asset to my team.

On getting up in the morning all you thought about was getting out into the street to see who you could play with or to see what was going on.

The main sight in our street at the top end was the gas tank. Its framework dominated but its size varied. Some days it was full and stretched to its full height and other days it had nearly disappeared, it was empty; up and down it went like a yo-yo. If you were up early enough you would see the milkman, Mr Joy. If you never saw him, evidence of his visit was sometimes on the floor, the manure his horse had left behind. I loved to see the horses and follow them around. They were so stately and gentle and no threat, unlike the motorcar and lorries that were dominating now. This was the end of an era; the few working horses left would soon be gone. The family of my school friend Frankie had a horse and this was kept in a stable in Window Lane, I went around a few times to see him. I was a bit nervous as we entered the stable, as it seemed dark and spooky. There were just a few shafts of light entering through gaps in the roof, and it was very quiet except for the gentle snorting of the horse. He seemed gigantic in his stall. It was a bit smelly but not offensive and everything about the experience was magic.
Hercules as the horse was known, pulled a coal cart so he had to be strong and well trained. He worked uncomplainingly, stopping and starting when told and seemingly oblivious to the people and traffic around him.

Railways And Accidents

Yes, transport was changing but I would see and travel on the trams. These disappeared when I was seven. I also travelled on the world famous overhead railway that ran from Dingle in the south to Seaforth in the north. I'm not sure if it was for business or pleasure but I remember being with my father and enjoying my ride, seeing the great sights from on high, of the river and its docks. There were hundreds of ships in the docks then and they seemed to go on for mile after mile.

The other mode of transport prevalent then was the steam train. If the docks of Garston were its heart then the railways were its arteries. Garston was surrounded and criss-crossed by railway lines. It is a source of pride to Garstonians that you cannot enter the centre of Garston unless you go over or under a bridge. Famous railway companies like L.M.S., Cheshire Lines, Great Western and Liverpool Corporation were represented everywhere.

We were warned to keep away from the railway lines and many horror stories were told to us. Being surrounded and living cheek by jowl with them they were a legitimate place to play and explore. Most of the trains were quite slow, just moving local freight, so you could hear and see them coming, which gave you time to move out of the way. The passenger trains were a bit quicker but the lines were protected by fences and by railway men. A great joy and memory for lots of people was to stand on a bridge as a steam train whistled and puffed underneath, then you would be enveloped in a mountain of steam as you shouted and danced in the cloud.

The freight lines where not protected by fencing and they ran from the docks to the factories. One of the lines ran to the match works where they carried logs for the manufacture of

Above: Garston railway lines, of which there were ninety three miles of track.

the matches. A walking right of way crossed this line at a point called the cinder path. This ran between the "under the bridge" community and the "Speke Road Gardens" community, which were tenements of five storeys. One of the games we played called chicken was when the train ran across the cinder path it lumbered so slowly we would duck underneath the train and come out the other side. One day when I wasn't there, a lad from the tenements was playing this prank when his shirt got caught under a wheel and he lost most of his arm. This then was a true horror story, told to us by teachers, as when I saw the lad he had one sleeve empty in his coat.

As with all children we suffered injuries while playing, some more serious than others. I remember a girl from York Street who spilt a pan of boiling water down her neck and she suffered terrible burns and scarring. Another lad stood on a plank and it sprang up and hit him in the eye. He lost the eye as the wood had a nail in the end.

Bonfire Night

I myself suffered another serious injury. November 5th was a big night, commonly called bonfire night to celebrate the burning of Guy Fawkes who had tried to blow up Parliament years before.

Our gang, called the Window Lane Mob, started to collect wood and anything that would burn, weeks before. We built our bonfire on an empty piece of wasteland in Window Lane but there was a problem. Other street gangs would steal your wood and wreck your bonfire and we would do the same to them, so there were some battles. The York Street gang were our rivals. Their bonfire was spectacular as it was in between two houses where once a house separated them. The house had been bombed in the war and had left a gap in the street. The fire engines would come and put it out, as it was dangerous to the occupants of the adjacent houses.

We were discouraged from taking part in "Bommie Night" but mostly we escaped and got out the house to join in.

There were all kinds of fireworks on show, rockets that went up with a spectacular whoosh then a bang and sometimes an explosion of colour. Bangers, which were just that, Catherine wheels which you nailed to a door, set alight and watched as they spun around throwing off sparks and light in all directions. Roman Candles that shot out single explosions one after the other and lit up the night. Ripraps were fireworks that exploded and jumped erratically all over the place.

All of these were dangerous if misused and this is what happened to me once. I was collecting bonfire wood. I had my wellington boots on when I came across a girl from school that had fireworks. She started lighting them and this was a great free show until she threw a Banger at me that unfortunately went down my wellington boot and exploded. As there was nowhere for the explosion to go except inside my boot, it blew a hole in my foot. I ran home, screaming, with my foot smoking and the skin on my foot blackened and falling off around the wound on my instep. My mum nearly fainted but she eventually got me into one of the young ones prams and wheeled me up to Garston hospital once again. As I was now ten years old I was more worried that my mates would see me in the pram than the hole in my foot.

Seasons of Life

I think if you live in the country you are more likely to be in touch with the seasons because it was necessary for the weather to be right for planting, growing and harvesting of crops. The seasons for us were divided into cricket and football seasons, and also the great Christian celebrations of Christmas and Easter. There was also bonfire night, duck apple night, pancake Tuesday and May Day. After Guy Fawkes Night, the next great festival was Christmas.

In school it was still very much celebrated as the birth of the baby Jesus. We were told the story of Joseph and Mary fleeing to Bethlehem for the birth of Christ, and then being unable to find room at the inn they were forced to go to a stable to have the baby. The angels, stars, shepherds, three wise men and the manger were all a big part of the story. It was always snowing and Jesus was wrapped in swaddling clothes and animals were looking on the scene with the shepherds.

We would start practising carols and decorating the tree in the classroom, and make the decorations from rings of coloured paper. Also we would make a frieze, which would go, right around the classroom. This would be a snow scene with trees, stars, stables and Father Christmas.

It was a very exciting time and I think it was all the better for us because like everyone else in the fifties, it was an austere period with not much expected. At Christmas, with the lights, singing, tidings of joy and presents to look forward to, it was a period of plenty in the year of shortages.

We would be taken to the Grotto in Evans', a local shop in Garston Village. This was a magical event and you got a present off Father Christmas at the end of it. The walk to Evans' was so exciting, wrapped up to keep warm, the crunch of your feet on ice or snow, your warm breath making steam in the freezing air and the shops festooned with lights and decorations.

The grotto in the shop seemed gigantic, you entered a cave-like entrance, inside were snow scenes with animals, seven dwarfs, Snow White and the handsome prince all glittering and smiling; transporting us to another world. Father Christmas sat on his chair, we sat on his knee, if we felt brave enough, and some were not brave enough and screamed at the funny man in a red suit, with a long white beard that spoke in a deep voice.

Above: St Mary's Road where the grotto was.

The days and weeks seemed to drag on forever before Christmas Eve when we could hang up our stockings. Our house had a small tree on the dresser and just a few decorations, but it was enough to give us a taste of the big day.

As children you never gave much thought to where all these great things came from. We just knew they would turn up on the day. For years it was Santa Claus who brought the presents, but this was spoilt by bigger children, who said, "it was your dad who brought your presents". Still, this didn't spoil the excitement of the day. One year by accident, I did find some presents as I was rooting in the wardrobe but I think I was discovered so the presents disappeared. This concerned me but I was reassured that if we stopped rooting and searching they would reappear on the day.

The night before we put our stockings up, well we never really did, we just laid them on the fire-grate, which was marble so we couldn't hang them. We put a carrot out for Rudolph the red nosed reindeer and went to bed still wide-eyed and awake, listening for every sound. I swear one year I heard reindeer bells, if not, my imagination was working overtime.

We woke early, it was still dark, and I decided to get up. It was very cold but that didn't matter we were so excited. On opening the door and switching on the light, the room had been transformed into an Aladdin's cave of treasures all wrapped up in fancy paper. We started to open our own gifts that were neatly stacked in our own pile. At this time there were four piles, Patrick's, Timmy's, Keith's and my own.

Dad heard the noise downstairs and got up annoyed. He found me sat in the middle of the floor shivering with cold but still stuffing my face with chocolate. He chased us back to bed but not deterred I sneaked back down and found the handle of the door had been tied to the banister with rope. I went back to bed to get up at a more reasonable time.

Every year I asked for the same things, football kit, football boots and a ball. There they would be, all wrapped up as if they really did come from Father Christmas, and in a way they did. The cries of joy, as you opened your gifts was very real and it was hard to take it all in as you looked around at what others had got. Someone was always given a compendium of games with snakes and ladders, ludo, draughts and all kinds of dice and counters, soon lost, Books, crayons, motorcars, blow football, a conductor's outfit, sweets and chocolates. The stockings contained apples and tangerines. A veritable feast of goodies we were all grateful to receive.

It was a close call sometimes. I have since learned that some years it was as late as Christmas Eve when Dad and Mum would be rushing around Garston Market and the village getting the presents with his Christmas money.

No breakfast would be needed after all the sweets, but a fire would be lit to keep our bare backsides warm. After all the excitement we were washed, put into a new shirt and pants, shoes if we had got them and new coat, then taken to see the new baby Jesus in church.

Holy Trinity Church was just a short walk away in Banks Road. Sometimes you skidded on the ice or dodged the slush puddles of melting snow or just tramped through the snow.

I loved the church. It smelt, looked and was decorated, beautifully and God lived there in the tabernacle on the altar. The giant candles where lit, glorious flowers festooned the church. The statues all looked on with pious looks, and the baby Jesus was snug in his manger. The crib was wonderful. It had life-sized people or so it seemed to me; shepherds, the three wise men and of course the animals.

I stared at the stable and the straw on the floor, the poor baby, humble Mary and Joseph, and was taken over by the peace of the whole scene.

Television and Washing Machines

Things were getting better at the end of the '50s, there was plenty of work, a lot more in the shops and people became more affluent. Television became more common and we got our first one in 1959. This was black and white and only had two channels. There wasn't much for children, just children's hour. A few of the programmes I remember vaguely were Animal Magic, Blue Peter, Robin Hood and the Lone Ranger. In the afternoon, for younger children, there was Watch with Mother, and I still remember Bill and Ben the Flowerpot Men, Picture Book and Rag Tag and Bobtail.

About this time mum got her first washing machine. It never seemed to be off and always seemed to be chugging away in what we called the back kitchen. The back kitchen had a stone Belfast sink, a draining board, and a geyser for hot water, washing machine and a stand up kitchen cabinet.

An accident with the kitchen cabinet caused Patrick and myself to get another good telling off and a belt. If you wanted to reach the top shelf of the cabinet you climbed on the drop leaf door. I wanted jam and this was on the top shelf, so we climbed on the drop leaf. The cabinet became unbalanced and as it wasn't attached to the wall it just toppled over. This resulted in a tremendous crash as everything fell off the shelf and cupboard and smashed on the floor. There was bread, sugar, crockery and jam spread everywhere, but by a miraculous chance the cabinet itself stopped from hitting the floor before squashing us flat. The top had jammed against the kitchen back door, just feet from the hard tiled floor.

When mum heard the crash she rushed into the kitchen to find us covered in flour, jam and broken crockery and we cowered, terrified and lying on the floor. I think mum was relieved we

42

were still in one piece, but angry over the damage done. Then we heard the famous words again "wait until your father gets home". One of the good things that came out of this incident was that the cabinet was fastened to the wall.

School Lessons and Libraries

I was now becoming aware of the need to try hard in school. I liked school and I had a very enquiring mind and I enjoyed subjects that I thought interesting. I found art, music, geography and religious instruction most stimulating but found maths and science subjects rather cold and did struggle with them.

Above: Garston library, a Carnegie Library.

I also found staying quiet and behaving a problem sometimes and was too often guilty of being the class entertainer. I was torn between wanting to please the teachers who I mostly liked and keeping in with my peer groups who I played up to. As for my academic achievement, I varied, but through my years in junior school I always came near the top of the class in exams, but have to say maths let me down.

There was an undercurrent of rebellion with some of us. This took the form of "to be a real member of the gang you never took learning too seriously". To be a bookworm or a swot or teachers pet was a weakness and you were prone to bullying. Even though I liked school and wanted to learn I never gave it my all because of peer pressure. I'm afraid that in the schoolyard, to be a good footballer was to be sought after, to be a good fighter respected and to be cock of the school, heroic.

I was good at football, held my own in a scrap and kept well in with the cock, so I got on well in the law of the jungle. The gentler side of me loved to learn and especially to read. There was a little library not far from me on the corporation estate nicknamed "Hollywood". This estate had been built in the 1930s and because they had gardens, indoor toilets and bathrooms they were thought to be the height of luxury. They were a lot different from the streets that the estate ran alongside and it was quickly sought after as a place to live. To get to the library I went over the park and on to "Hollywood" where the library was. I joined with trepidation as I thought they would turn me down, being from the streets and not being posh. I know this is sad but somehow those were the thoughts I had, but luckily they accepted me and gave me a ticket. This was an entrance to a treasure-trove of books. At first I got every book about football and football players, then cricket players. I read biographies avidly and dreamed of the day when I would be a footballer. On getting a book I would clutch it to me and start to read it on the park. I would sit on a bench that looked over the bowling green and was transported to another world. I didn't like anyone to see me reading just in case they thought I was trying to be clever, it was my little secret.

One day I discovered novels. Now this was a revelation. Once I started to read a good novel I hated to put it down and in this way I discovered another world of adventure. I was there, my emotion and imagination fired as I sailed the seas, hid in caves, fought the good fight and saved the world. My favourites that I remember were Treasure Island by my No.1 author R.L. Stevenson and Kidnapped. Lorna Doone by R. D. Blackmore. I also read and enjoyed Dickens, 'Oliver Twist', 'A Tale of Two Cities' and 'David Copperfield'. Another book that I read in a day was H. Rider Haggard's 'King Solomon's Mines'.

I was always inquisitive, reading the Daily Express, especially the Gambols, a cartoon strip. I found a set of red backed books in the house, self help books designed to improve your confidence and knowledge. They were a bit beyond me as they were adult books, but I found the language fascinating and pored over them for hours, even though I could not really understand them.

Public debate fascinated me as well and the Pierhead in Liverpool had plenty of it. The Pier Head had its historic waterfront, its famous Liver Birds and Cunard Building, but its main purpose was as a landing stage. It was the main terminal for the ferries that ran between Wallasey, Birkenhead and Liverpool. It was a far busier river in the 50s and it had many great liners tied up there. I particularly remember the *Empress of Canada* and also the *Royal Iris* that belonged to the Isle of Man Steam Packet Company. We would explore the landing stage; I remember punching my name on a tin band with a punching machine. It was a hive of activity with people embarking or disembarking on the ships. The walk down to the landing stage, through a walkway as it moved slightly was always exciting. On the Pier Head plateau itself surrounded by statues and memorials, stood the preachers and orators, all trying to get their points of view across. We often stood and watched them perform and occasionally dad would ask them a challenging question and I would get a knot in my stomach as they started to debate. It usually ended up for us with an ice cream and this was heaven to me, the world seemed an endlessly magic place.

Cold Lino - Hot Porridge

It was hard at times, you had to be realistic, but it was all we knew and we had all we needed. Getting up for school was hard. I can't remember us having an alarm but once one was up we were all up. Winter could be severe and on rising the ice had decorated the windows and frozen your clothes. As your feet touched the cold lino you jumped with the shock. Moving quickly was the answer, throwing on clothes and gritting your teeth, then a dash downstairs for your breakfast. Breakfast was always porridge and this steamed away in the pan, at least it was hot as it was poured or plopped on your plate depending on whether it was watery or thick, I liked it thick with milk and sugar.

Additionally, a paraffin heater also provided heating and this spluttered away in the kitchen. It gave off a terrible smell sometimes, but this did not stop us crowding around it to get a warm, pushing and shoving each other to get near the flame. Very often we would singe our pants as we nearly sat on it, or you would heat up your legs that much when you moved it would burn, this made us hop around like a scalded cats, and if you needed to go down the yard to the toilet, that was another test of endurance. A quick dash down the yard, trousers down as quick as possible, wait for the cold of the seat to give you a start, no place to hang around, look for the crumpled paper hanging on a nail to finish the job and then flush. If it was particularly cold the cistern froze solid so no water flowed; just a clang as you pulled the chain but this was solved by a night light candle left lit, to stop the pipes and cistern freezing.

Once fed and dressed we were off to school only a short walk away. We never had a school uniform, all children just dressed as they liked, as long as you were clean and tidy. What you wore did not seem important then. There were no designer labels for fashion statements, no skitting of what you wore. It all seemed so much more egalitarian then. Most of the pupils came from the same working class background and never had the money for fashionable clothes; some just had enough to put clothes on your back. On arriving at the school you would mingle in the yard waiting for the hand bell to be rung. On cold days this couldn't come soon enough as you huddled in corners, faces buried in scarves and balaclavas. I remember going into the air raid shelter in the schoolyard for more shelter. This was out of bounds but we sneaked in, it stunk in there and was full of rubbish. When the bell rang we lined up in our classes and then entered the school in an orderly fashion, congregating in the hall for assembly. The school was always warm in winter; it hit you as soon as you walked in, the steam pipes being a favoured place to sit or lean and to get warm. The pipes went right around the school and this was the nearest any of us came to central heating.

Occasionally the school was cold when the boiler broke down and then we were sent home. The boiler was in the mysterious place underground where the caretaker lived and it seemed a scary place. Once the teacher told me to fetch the caretaker as a boy had been sick all over the floor. I felt a bit nervous about this request but could not say no, so off I went to the door of the cellar, opened it and crept down the stairs calling out to sir, "someone's been sick". I reached the bottom before he answered with a grunt "alright, I'll be there soon". He was sitting in the gloom smoking and reading a paper and he looked foreboding. Pupils were always sick and nearly every day you would see pools of vomit covered with sawdust, looking like cow pats.

Another job for the caretaker was mopping up blood after the many accidents that happened. A job I had in school was milk monitor and this task meant that me and another boy collected a crate of milk for distribution in the class. I liked this job as I drank a bottle before we returned to the classroom. The government felt this milk was necessary to give children the extra protein they might otherwise not get and in a lot of cases this was true. One day, bringing the crate back we slipped and fell. Tony O'Malley gashed his knee on the broken glass; there was blood everywhere and screams from the girls. I ran for the caretaker as the teacher gave first aid.

Room was now scarce at home, I spent more time in the front parlour with the musical instruments, especially the guitar. I strummed away, sometimes too hard, trying to do rock and roll, breaking strings in the bargain. I also liked to draw and I had a book on teach yourself to draw; I spent hours trying to draw an eye.

Green Oasis

I still spent more time out than in, on the park, and as mother had her hands full she didn't mind.

Below: Bowling Green, Garston Park.

I loved to watch the Crown Green bowling. It fascinated me, the way the bowls rolled and bent as they travelled across the green. The men and women seemed very old but cheerful, as they went from corner to corner with their bowls. I loved the sound of one bowl hitting another, sometimes going into the ditch, and if it landed by me I would roll the ball back.

It was sacrilege to step on the green if you were a child and the park keeper would chase you. The odd occasion I did step on the green it felt like soft sponge beneath my feet, it was like a luxury carpet and the colour was a beautiful green, decorated with stripes the green keeper had lovingly mown.

On a sunny day I sat on a bench surrounded by trees and lovely flowerbeds. The birds would be singing, the sun blazing down and the butterflies and bees foraging and flitting among the multicoloured flowers. I had my first inkling of the majesty of nature in this green oasis amongst the streets. As I dreamt on the bench I felt a deep peace and a feeling of utter contentment. I would watch for hours and if I got thirsty I drank from the fountain in the park. You just turned a knob and the water would trickle out of a spout, all for free, and it was the most thirst quenching, cooling drink I ever had. At the bottom of the fountain was a half moon bowl which caught the over spill, this was for thirsty dogs. A lot of the time around the fountain it was muddy, even in the hottest weather.

1950s End, 60s Begin

This was an era that would light up the world, and a main part of that change would be the Merseybeat. The Beatles would be the biggest group of all time and would change popular music forever. But on the 7th November 1957 they were just a bunch of lads starting off together and on this date they played the "Wilson Hall" in Garston. The reason I remember this date is because it was my 7th birthday and I was hanging around outside Wilson Hall as I often did, just to watch what went on and maybe bum some money and listen to the muffled music. This night these scruffy lads got out of a van and as we always did, I asked, "could we mind it Mister?" No, get lost, you little B's said one of the band carrying his guitar. "Ah, go on," said I "It's my birthday". On hearing this he laughed and threw me a penny. Years later I realised this was Mr John Lennon himself, one of the Beatles, I like to think it was anyway.

The sixties would mean great changes for me as well. I now became aware that I would be moving on to a senior school when I was eleven. I did not know which school because of something called the Eleven Plus. I was quite bright at school and had a reasonable chance of passing the Eleven plus if I tried, so the teacher said. I was now in my last year at Holy Trinity and was in the top stream class with some of the swots. The problem was I could not see any reason to pass the Eleven Plus. What was the advantage? I could only see problems. The school was too far. What about my mates? My football might suffer.

Yes. My football was still the most important area of my life and to me this was where my future lay.

I had no role models like doctors, lawyers, bankers or university lecturers. This type of people was non-existent "Under the Bridge". My role models and heroes were footballers and boxers, and they seemed to be around me, and their life seemed attainable without passing the Eleven Plus.

One hero lived at the top of our street. He was Mr Albert Dunlop who was the Everton goalkeeper and he had a car. I saw him visit his parents once when I stood outside and I got his autograph.

I did try in my final year but not very hard. I didn't do homework once so when the exam took place it didn't have any relevance to me, as I wanted to go to the local secondary school because they had a good football team.

Consequently, I did not pass the exam and got my wish.

The funny thing was, I felt a slight disappointment on not passing, as I did not like the feeling of failure. I think if I had known the importance society put on this exam and on the senior school you went to, I would have been even more disappointed. I was very pleased, years later, when this exam was abolished. I felt and did experience the major and unfair difference the failure at this exam at such an early age made to the rest of your life.

Sporting Success

One success I did have in the final year in junior school was to play in the football team.

I was thrilled to be picked and played with a passion for the success of our school team. What a great year it was. I do not remember a defeat and we went on to win a trophy and play the final at Bellfield, Everton's training ground.

The school colours were green and white and the school shirts were green and white with hooped socks, a bit like Celtic, the great Glasgow team. On the way to the final we played Banks Road School and they played in blue like Rangers the other great Glasgow team, this turned out to be a great match.

The rivalry was terrific because it was a local derby and we knew and were friends with many of their boys. In this match we beat them 2-0 and I scored one goal I can remember to this day. My father was there that day as he was at a lot of matches. Another spectator was one of our priests, Father Darragh, who was a most kindly man. I vividly remember him after our cup final success, coming into the dressing room with a tray full of cream cakes. The boys soon scoffed these but curiously, I was so excited at our success, I did not feel like a cake, for the first time in my life. I clutched on to the medal I had won and kept looking at it. It was only a little silver shield but to me it was a Kings bounty and I was proud to show everyone I met. I still had hold of it the next morning at assembly, when the headmaster announced our win.

Above: Holy Trinity Cup winning football team.

I still have a photograph of the team resplendent in green and white, I remember this even though the photo taken at the time is in black and white. I also have a photograph taken on the same day of the cricket team.

The cricket team had also won a cup and apart from one or two, it was the same lads from the football. On the day of the pictures, we just made a quick change from our football kit to cricket and that meant for most of us, just putting on a white shirt. Mr Kelly congratulated me on mine, as it was so white, he then told a couple of the lads off for having no white shirt. In the cricket picture, two boys held bats and in the centre the wicket keeper held the cup in his gloved hands. He also was the only one with cricket pads on.

I liked cricket although I didn't much like the hard cork cricket ball. It always seemed to hit you on your fingers or on your legs, or, on one occasion, on the head. We did wear padded gloves but these were threadbare and not much protection. We also wore pads on our legs but as we only had a couple the batsmen only had one each. If you were lucky you got hit on the leg with the pad but I often got hit on my unprotected leg. We did not have any cricket boxes which protected your privates so if you were unlucky enough to be hit there it made your eyes water. As a batsman I never knew many strokes but I was hard to get out as I stood in front of the wicket with a dead straight bat and just blocked the ball with anything. Not many fours were hit and we used a tactic called tip it and run. This meant that if you hit the ball with anything you just ran as fast as you could hope not to be ran out. It used to work for a bit but once the other team worked it out they were ready to run us out so we would then change tactics by giving the ball a slog as hard as you could.

Goal Posts and Cricket Wickets

We drew goal posts on the gable end wall at the end of the street, and cricket wickets where the gas pipes came out of the ground at just the right height and width for a wicket, then all we had to do was draw the bails across the top, and the street was just the right size across for a cricket pitch. The only problem for us was windows! And not surprisingly we often got chased to the park by our parents or neighbours.

We played a lot of games in the street, such as marbles or ollies as we called it, hopscotch, and billy kick the can, rallevo, jacks and pitching toss. We liked to play in the back entries or jiggers as we called them. The back jiggers were a veritable maze and linked all the streets in the area. We used them as shortcuts to our mates' houses, and for some suspicious characters they were a way of moving around unseen. Of a night we would run up and down, hollering and banging on the back doors. The dogs would bark and the people curse and if you were caught you got a clip around the ear. We also tormented the bigger lads who might be doing a bit of courting with their girlfriends in various degrees of clinches. You were quick when you were chased. We thought them proper idiots kissing girls who we still shunned, but years later we would be doing the same thing.

Above: Derby Street Gable end, where we put our goal posts and wickets.

Birth and Dying

I used one of these shortcuts to visit Grandma who still lived in the house my mother was born in, in Ultonia Street. I liked Grandma, she was kind and always gave us 2p as pocket money and that was enough to buy sweets such as a penny arrow bar and still have change. I sometimes went on a message for her to buy some boiled ham or the paper. I remember going to the local the "Canterbury" for a jug of ale.

There was no problem getting served, you went in the side door and there was a serving hatch in the back of the bar. I loved the smell and the atmosphere of the pub; it seemed so bright and cheery compared to the streets outside. I carried the frothing jug back to gran, careful not to spill any but I did take a sip once and was intrigued by the bitter malty taste. Gran always wore a pinny, a sort of flowery overall with pockets at the front in which she kept her purse, and on delivery she would give me my reward.

Gran's house was a treasure trove; the parlour fascinated me as I stared at the various bronze statues, dogs, and a roman soldier with a spear. She had a beautiful glass case with lots of little treasures, bone china, glass trinkets, ivory carvings and fancy ornaments. I do remember a glass dome with a nude statue inside.

Maternal grandfather had died a couple of years earlier. He had an adventurous life having been in both the army and the merchant navy. When he finally settled down he worked on Garston docks. He liked a pint and football and used to take me walks up the shore.

When I was still a toddler he took me out in my pram up the shore. This day somehow, I lost a shoe, a brand new shoe as mother told him. He was sorry he upset mum, as he knew the shoes were expensive to buy. He died relatively young at 57 years from a heart attack. My mum was heartbroken as she was very close to him. I remember seeing her crying and didn't know why, but dad told us about grandpa and I had a cry.

About this time, Daniel was born upstairs in Derby Street, that made it five boys. I don't remember the build up or any talk of a new baby, so it was a surprise. There was just a bit of kerfuffle. Mum went upstairs; the midwife arrived, she was a "Mrs Williams" and safely delivered the new addition.

I was not surprised, shocked, sad, glad or mad about a new brother, it was just a fact and I accepted it. But it was necessary to build up my own world. I lived more outdoors and lost myself in my obsessions, especially football. Mum was more distracted now than ever, up to her neck in nappies, bottles, washing and cooking – she could have done with a maid. She tried to give us the time we needed but this proved impossible with five boys to nurture. So I got out of the way to the park mostly. What to wear was never an issue except for the essentials like keeping dry or wearing warm clothes in winter or cool clothes in summer. Fashion never came into it. Just old clothes for school, and don't wear your good shoes for football. These rules were often broken, as I couldn't be bothered to change, and ended up with no good clothes and scuffed shoes and socks around my ankles.

Above: Now we are five boys.

I sometimes wore pumps as we called them – black canvas lightweights designed for games. These were the forerunners of trainers but a lot cheaper. They didn't last long, I even had plastic red sandals and they fell apart at the first sign of a ball.

Wellington boots were good in the rain but were no good for running or football and they left red welts around your calves were the rubber chafed your bare legs, your socks always ended up in a knot in the toe end of your boots.

Football boots were obviously the best for kicking a ball but these were no good on the street because of the slippery studs. The boots were of a robust heavy design with great heavy toecaps, and leather nailed in studs. I always wanted new football boots, but I made do with a new pair of white laces and putting dubbin on my old ones.

From a Junior to a Senior

I learnt in school I had been allocated a place in Blessed John Almond, the local secondary school (later to be called St. John Almond as the Saint went up in the Church's esteem). I only had a couple of months in junior school left. Nothing left much of an impression in my last year except the Christmas party where I performed a song "The Worm at the Bottom of the Garden" and also won a box of chocolates in a quiz. I still remember the answer "Canterbury" but I can't remember the question. I ate a lot of food none of which I took. I did take a plate and spoon however just in case.

The summer holidays couldn't come soon enough. My time at Holy Trinity was coming to an end. I was leaving with mixed feelings. I would miss the school, but I was looking forward to senior school. All children want to grow up as soon as possible and I was no exception. I would remember the good teachers and try to forget the bad. I had made some good friends, had some education, a chapter closed in my life, a chapter that loomed large in my memory far exceeding its four years length.

I was now eleven and ready to explore the world. All summers seemed to be sunny and hot in our childhood memories and winters were cold and it always snowed at Christmas. Well that year 1962 was like that. It seemed to be sunny and hot a lot and it definitely was a very cold and icy winter. First the summer holidays, at that time father worked for a company that delivered food to restaurants, hotels and top class eating establishments. One perk of the job was that on my eleventh birthday the chef at the company made me a cake all decorated like a football pitch, it didn't look like a football pitch for long as we all devoured it. Another perk was some days dad would take me on deliveries with him. I enjoyed this a lot and got to see a bit of the countryside. One part I didn't like was the live fish and lobster in a big bucket in the back of the van. I always felt sorry for them knowing they would be on someone's dinner plate later on. At one posh hotel the chef took us in the back and gave us a dinner and a sweet, never have I tasted such a dish as that tasted to me then.

Left: Dad with mates having a break at Dunlops.

I think dad liked the freedom of the road more than working in a factory. His attempts to work indoors were not successful; he had worked at Dunlop's Rubber Factory, Tate & Lyle and the Bottle Works but had not settled. Our street was cheek by jowl with the factories and docks. You were well aware of the industry from the moment you woke up to the time you went to bed.

Garston Industry

In the morning there were a series of hooters, sirens and klaxons to call the workers to work. There was the rumble of industry in the background all the time, you got so you didn't notice it. There were smells and terrible odours pervading the atmosphere and some days they were stronger than others. These smells came from the gas works as the coal was turned to gas, and the residue was piled into Coke Mountains, not the drink but coal sucked of all its goodness, to be left like burnt cinders.

Above: Logs for the matchworks unloading on Garston Docks.

Another bad smell was the tannery where raw cowhides were turned into leather. This process used all kinds of chemicals and lime to make the leather and the funny thing was the finished product, sole leather, saddle leather, and shoe leather had a wonderful odour.

One other smell I liked was wood and there were mirror works and picture frame manufacturers in Window Lane. As you passed a lovely smell of wood shavings would waft through the air. Also there were timber merchants and builders where you would hear the sound of circular saws whizzing away, throwing sawdust all around which on hot days would hang in the air and you could taste the dry woodiness of it all.

Goods from all over the world came into the docks, unloaded by an army of men, and giant cranes stood guard over the docks like Meccano soldiers. These goods gave off all kinds of odours from the smell of coal dust to the smells of timber and bananas.

These industries surrounded the "Under the Bridge" community and most of the people worked locally. As they went to work it was like an army of ants. If you stood in Window Lane on their return in the evening as the buzzers went, it was like a football crowd coming up from the factories.

Most of the men wore flat caps and heavy boots, scarves around their necks and overalls. The women wore headscarves, overalls and heeled shoes. Not everyone dressed the same of course, the girls in the shops dressed differently from factory girls. Men on the docks dressed differently from tannery workers, but the fact was that all workers had a distinct mode of dress or uniform in some cases. A point of interest was the future General Secretary of the T & G once lived a few streets away in York Street, in a two up and two down house. He would end up with great influence during the Labour era and was part of the beer and butties conferences with the Prime Minister in Downing Street. One thing about Jack Jones was he was a man of integrity and could have become Lord Jones, but he chose to become leader of the pensioners when he retired and became a pensioner himself.

A good man of Garston, we used to wonder if he was related to mother who was another Jones of Garston, but we never did find out.

Senior School and Big Boys

The summer holidays came to an end; I was now ready to begin my life as a senior in a new school, "Blessed John Almond Secondary Modern School. I was going from being a big boy in a little school to being a little boy in a big school. It was 1962 and I was eleven as I started in the first year of the senior school.

I remember my first day because it was the first time I wore my school uniform. I had a new blazer, new hardwearing shoes, and a new shirt, short trousers – I wore short trousers until I was 14, unheard of these days.

The school was Blessed John Almond situated in Horrocks Avenue, about half a mile away. This was close enough to walk. I could go by two routes, either under the bridge or up the cinder path, depending on my mood. The school had feeder schools in Garston, Aigburth, Allerton and Woolton. It was a new school having been built at the end of the fifties.

It was a mixed school, boys and girls in the first year. The boys still had no interest in the girls and they were treated with indifference, but that would soon change.

It was a Roman Catholic school; of that there was no doubt. There were statues and pictures of Saints and Popes and Cardinals around the school. We attended assembly every morning for prayers, and on a Wednesday we had mass.

The classrooms all had a crucifix on the wall and two of the teachers were nuns. It was an impressive school with a large gymnasium, woodwork and metalwork rooms, science labs and cookery classrooms. It had the lot, and to cap it all a massive playing field for football, athletics, cricket and games. The only problem with the playing field was the undulating hills, you couldn't find a level pitch anywhere, and it was like the Himalayas! Still, after a schoolyard in the last school this was great. Finally we had modern changing rooms with showers. Quite a novelty seeing a lot of us never even had a bath in the house.

I settled in well and once again enjoyed myself, made friends easily and was determined to make my mark as a footballer. Sport was not the top priority with the school, academic lessons were and so was discipline. But in my time in the school we were lucky in that we had a couple of teachers who encouraged sport and gave up a lot of their spare time.

I made new friends and enjoyed the new challenges. I had one or two hiccups. I had a run in with the teacher who didn't like my attitude, which was a bit too chatty for her. I would never understand why you had to be quiet and serious when studying. Surely a bit of light heartedness would make learning more fun and we would be more co-operative. My first teacher, Miss Corr, was very Victorian and stern but by the end of my first year we had made friends. I think she realised I wanted to learn and was not insolent as she first thought. The second hiccup was a new lad. He started after us and soon wanted to throw his weight around. He was from the town and wanted to teach us locals a lesson. Inevitably, he went to me because I was the talker and told him to get lost. He said "I'll get you at dinner time". One thing, he kept his word and soon we were rolling round the playground with the usual crowd around us baying for blood. Anyway, I gave as good as I got, the fight was stopped, no winner and two losers.

When I went home mum went mad. My coat was ruined and I had a big eye. I don't know what she was most angry about. Anyway, she wanted to go up to the school to complain about this bully, and this she did, much to my consternation and protest. When she saw the teacher, the other boy was brought in to show mother that it had not been one-sided and he had two black eyes.

Freezing Winter Of 62-63

The first few months raced by, the darkness of winter was coming fast, the leaves of autumn were falling as the trees were preparing to sleep through the winter, and what a winter it would be. 1962-63 was one of the worst winters of the century, it seemed to last forever.

At home the problem was to keep warm. The house froze, the toilet froze and we froze. The fire was the only source of heat except for a paraffin heater in the kitchen. The bedrooms were the coldest rooms and the front parlour was shut down. We had a coal fire and this took time to start in the morning, as the ashes had to be emptied from the night before, the grate had to be cleaned, and a new fire prepared. First, we had to crumple paper, then sticks and if we were lucky we then added coal. We often didn't have coal, as it was expensive. Sometimes I went round to the shop and got fire sticks to start the fire, and coal bricks to burn. More often than not we burned wood. This came from different sources, mainly from dad's work, old crates, which sparked a lot when burning. It was fun as sparks shot out of the fire and burned holes in the lino. Blocks of wood were sometimes bought or we would go to the sawmill and get offcuts. There was coal to be found up the shore in the mud, this was from the coal boats that used Garston Docks, any spillage would go in the dock and be washed out by the tide, to be deposited later on the shoreline. You could also pinch coke from the Gas Works but you had to be careful in case you got buried under the coke mountain. Old shoes, lino, wood, coal and coke all went up in flames in an effort to keep warm. No wonder Garston disappeared under a blanket of smog. There were days when you couldn't see your hands in front of you. These fogs were commonly known as "pea soupers". The air was thick with industrial smoke and all the houses poured out their own pollution through the chimneys, which sometimes caught fire, and we would all stare up at the sparking black soot as it blazed out of the chimney and enveloped us all. I loved the feel of the "pea soupers", the stillness, the secrecy, and the silence. There was something eerie about it and the haunting sound of the ships on the river as they sounded their foghorns to warn other ships. All this added to the atmosphere of danger and magic.

Above: Tracks in the snow, Garston Docks.

It was so cold the toilet froze and even the one tap in the kitchen froze up. I remember my dad using a blowtorch to unfreeze the pipes.

More blankets and coats went on the beds and you snuggled up to anyone in bed, and watched your breath as it froze even indoors, as you breathed it out. The windows had beautiful patterns of frost traced on them; even the pee bucket froze. You hopped on the cold lino when you got out of bed and threw your clothes on which stood up stiff and frozen in the corner.

Above: A happy girl enjoying the freeze, showing Holy Trinity Church, Banks Road School and the Gasworks in the background.

A quick splash of water on your face and you were ready for the world. Wrapped up as best you could to face the onslaught of winter. Often you would get up to a fresh fall of snow, sometimes up to three feet deep, lying in great drifts around the street. We sometimes earned a bit of extra money by going snow clearing outside people's houses, making a path by shovelling and brushing the snow into piles either side of the path. Snowballs were the favourite game. I got carried away once and nearly got frostbite. I ended up screaming with pain as I tried to get my hands warm and dry. After that I never really liked cold hands. Slide making was another pastime; it took hours to get the perfect glass finish of an ice slide. We would spend hours slipping and sliding on one leg, two legs or your bottom, trying to get the furthest distance. On a good slide you could go for fifty yards or more.

Snow had the effect of making even the streets look nice; the park was a winter wonderland after a fresh fall of snow. The trees laced with white, the branches bent with the weight, the ground a blanket of white. No boundaries visible. I felt guilty stepping into the snow, spoiling its pristine whiteness.

The night took on a muffled quietness. Everything seemed to slow down and be at peace. The flakes would fall to the ground like feathers adding to the silence. Only the crunch of your shoes in the snow made a sound. The song "Silent Night" was the perfect song for the snow-silenced nights. The moon and stars seemed to shine brighter on clear nights and your breath froze in the air.

Dad made us a sledge complete with tin strips on the runners to make it go faster. Everywhere was flat except for a hill on the Hollywood estate where you could toboggan, free falling down the slope. It was full of all sorts of sledges and all sorts of kids competing to go the fastest and furthest.

Winter seemed to last forever from one thaw to the next snowfall. I didn't play much football, in fact the school had no first year team so there was no competitive football for me in my own age group, but later on in that year, I played some games for the 2nd year. I was younger and smaller but I made up for any disadvantage with greater skill

In the February of 1963, our family was about to be made complete. My mother was expecting twins. I had no idea of the implication of this. It seemed perfectly normal to welcome new babies every so often. For the next few weeks, I spent a lot of time farmed out, as mum had a long spell in hospital.

The babies were born prematurely, a boy Peter and a girl Angela, the first girl after six boys. She was well when she was born but Peter was not well and dad had been told he might not live. They were both small and in incubators but Peter was the weakest. We all prayed a lot and I got the school assembly to pray for them. It must have worked as they both made good progress and were home after a few weeks. So that was it, now seven children and two adults all squashed into our little house in Derby Street.

One of the ways we made room was to get bunk beds for me, and my brother Patrick. I slept on top and this was all right until I was ill and unfortunately I was sick all over Patrick, who looked up just as I vomited down. Three others, Tim, Keith and Daniel shared a double bed and that made five in one room. This was no problem. You just got on with it and accepted what came along.

Seismic Changes

I was growing up and changing a lot now which was traumatic enough for me without the massive changes in the world, a lot of these changes were centred on the great city of Liverpool.

You became aware of the phenomena called the "Beatles", a pop group that grew up in Liverpool and nurtured its sound in the "Cavern", a cellar in Matthew Street. All of the band, John, Paul, Ringo and George were from the south end of the city. The first song I heard was "Love Me Do". I liked that especially the harmonica John played. Then the massive hit "Please Please Me" went to the top of the charts. The rest, as they say, was history. The whole "Merseybeat" sound swept the world with groups like "Gerry and the Pacemakers", "Searchers", "Merseybeats", Billy J Kramer and lots more. Also a girl appeared in the Cavern at this time collecting coats. Her name was Cilla Black and she became a top singer and then a famous television star.

You felt strangely proud of your association with the explosion of interest in Liverpool and for a few years it just got bigger and bigger. Our hair got longer and longer and so began the teenage rebellion that rumbled on right through the sixties.

In Liverpool you either supported the REDS "Liverpool F.C." or the BLUES "Everton F.C.". I was a Liverpool fan and had been even when they were in the Second Division. In the early sixties they were promoted to the First Division and for the next thirty years they were the most successful team ever. They had a charismatic manager by the name of Bill Shankly, who rebuilt Liverpool and in so doing, became a legend in his lifetime. He had great determination and a great wit. One of his famous sayings was "Football is not a matter of life or death, it is more important than that". We heard of players like St. John, the giant Ronnie Yeats, Roger Hunt and all great players. I hardly watched the match because I was always playing football on Saturday and Sunday, but when I did go it was a tremendous experience. The stadium seemed gigantic, the colours and noise were mind-blowing, and games so exciting as the crowd in the Kop surged and swayed like a Mersey tide as they followed the ebb and flow of the football. When there was a goal the roof lifted off with the roar. It was said that the roar of the Kop was worth a goal to Liverpool before kick off. The Kop became as famous as the team for their vocal support but especially for their singing. They made the song "You'll Never Walk Alone" world famous and it became a football anthem forever linked with Liverpool. The Kop even sang Beatle songs like "She Loves You, Yeah, Yeah, Yeah". It was a great time to be a Liverpudlian, not only because of the success but also because of the great surge of pride in all things Merseyside or Merseypride as they said.

The third strand of the massive shifts in society came from religion, more specifically our religion, Roman Catholic. An institution that was noted for its conservatism and had hardly changed in thousands of years had declared Vatican Council to discuss the future role of the church in the world. Pope John XXIII instigated these changes, as he felt that the church needed to look at itself. It did not impact immediately on our lives or worship except when we prayed for its success. Eventually the changes in the church were enormous. The main change for me was the liturgy was now in our own language instead of in Latin, I could now understand what was said at mass. There were a lot of people against the changes, but I think the vast majority welcomed them and felt the Council's decisions breathed new life into the Church. These changes in the Church took time to percolate through our school, which was still very much a traditional catholic school in its ethos and aims.

Mr McGarvey and Sister Gertrude

The headmaster, Mr McGarvey was a wonderful man, well liked and respected by pupils and teachers alike. His deputy head was Sister Gertrude and she ruled the school with a rod of iron. But for all this show of harshness I found her not too bad, a true case of her "bark was worse than her bite". I could be a bit cheeky but she responded sometimes with a smile that melted the harsh exterior. I felt six feet tall when she chose me to go on a message for her to Garston Market that was over the road from the school. I do believe she felt that the harsh discipline exterior was necessary to run the school, because after all, there were some very naughty or even bad lads who did need a tight rein on them, or they would have run wild. Mr McGarvey was such a gentleman in the best sense of the word but he did not have the necessary stature to engender respect in a hard way. The school had to be a safe and secure environment for all the children and Sister Gertrude made sure of this. So in a way this was the most Christian thing she could do.

Above: Football team with Mr McGarvey on far right.

I enjoyed my first year in the school. There were new challenges and subjects. We were being prepared for the world outside, so we were allowed to take woodwork and metalwork classes. I found the smell of the woodwork class nice, it reminded me of the sawmills in Garston. I liked to saw; chisel and plane wood because it felt creative. The only problem was the need for precision and this I often got wrong, that meant a bad joint like a tenon or mortice spoilt the job. Because of this I never excelled at woodwork. As for metal work I didn't like the smell of it as it reminded me of Blackwells, the smelting works in Banks Road. It smelt of oil, burnt coke and grease. I made pokers, tea caddy spoons; shoe lasts and often burnt myself. As the metal heated up sparks flew, as you hammered the metal into shape, just like a blacksmith.

At the end of my first year in senior school, as in every year, I sat a test in class. I came about middle and had no serious problems. I had excelled in sport and coped with the change from child to budding adult. Now like all school children I looked forward to breaking up and to all the things I had planned for the long summer holiday.

Up the Shore

One of the things I loved was to explore and play up the shore. This was the coast line along the Mersey between Garston docks and Hale Lighthouse, a distance of 5 miles. This area to me was heaven. I had my happiest memories up the shore.

Living in the streets surrounded by industry and noise, and all the traffic and people and hustle and bustle, it was a relief to be able to escape into the fields and coastline along the Mersey.

I only had to walk through a few streets then alongside a brook down Brunswick Street, past the allotment and there it was, the first field looking across the sparkling Mersey.

I was never bored because no two days were the same. The weather was the biggest factor in the mood. You could have lovely hot still days and the river would be placid like a millpond, just lapping on the mud shore. On a breezy day the river would chop up its white horses, rushing and crashing on the sandbanks. On stormy days, which I loved, the river would rush in, roaring and racing and smashing into the sandstone wall, which ran alongside the airport. The clouds always seemed to imitate the sea. On gentle days fluffy clouds just hung in the sky, barely floating. On breezy days the clouds would race across the sky switching the sun on and off and casting shadows on the sea. On stormy days everything went mad, the massive grey clouds, the rain ' throwing it down', and the wind smashing the clouds into each other so they disintegrated and merged into one.

Above: Garston Shore, looking out to river.

I sat for hours just surveying these scenes and never got tired of the sights. On a hot day the river shimmered in the heat, a haze rising up to merge with the sky so sea, sky and land became one.

I lost myself in the long grass and just dreamed. The grasshoppers serenaded me as they hopped around clicking their legs as they jumped. Butterflies of all colours and sizes, red admirals, common blue and white cabbage butterflies and most of all the meadow brown, flitted from plant to plant. I would watch intently the spiders, beetles and creepy crawlies of all descriptions as they foraged amongst the undergrowth.

Above: Shipbreakers yard, Garston Shore.

I never put a name to anything as a boy. I just watched everything and enjoyed them all. If I went with my friends I did less watching and more exploring. There was a breaker's shipyard alongside the Bottle Works just past the docks. There we would explore the old ships taking our lives in our hands as we climbed onto the ships, jumping over the holds and from boat to boat. If we fell we would fall 20 feet into the mud below or onto the skeletal steel remains of the ship. The tide would come in swirling below, encircling the ships, and cutting us off from the land. No problem for intrepid explorers like us, we just took our shoes off and waded to shore. The water and mud concealed hidden dangers. I cut my feet more than once on broken glass hidden in the mud. I would wash the blood away, put a dock leaf on like a plaster and just carry on.

The shore in Garston was mostly mud and rocks. The further up you went away from the docks and industry it became cleaner and sandy. We used to wade in the mud looking under rocks for crabs and shrimps. If you dived in the mud you could slide for miles, we were always caked in mud and when it dried it went hard and then you could pick it off, or if you never had a costume, leave the mud on around the private bits. We never realised the danger of disease in the polluted mud, but most of us were very healthy, probably immune to anything in the mud. Maybe that's why Garston lads were known as "Mud Men", a tag of affection rather than ridicule.

When the tide came in I moved fast, as I still could not swim and it was easy to get caught out as the tide rushed in and the current was very strong. I decided then that I must learn to swim soon. I loved the shore and if I wanted to explore the sandbanks or go out in a boat it would be necessary to be able to swim. On land I would go for long walks with my mates. The path alongside the airport then across the farmers' fields past Speke Hall would stretch for miles, sometimes we got as far as Hale Lighthouse. The path alongside the airport ran for part of the way on the clay boulder cliffs and seemed to move year by year as the cliffs were eroded away and often collapsed into the sea. The flora of the cliff hid the path at times; this was mainly bracken and drifts of wild flowers. After the cliffs of the airport was a large brick building called the Boathouse, which belonged to Liverpool Sailing Club? It had a brick and concrete slipway and jetty that stretched well out into the Mersey. I liked to watch the yachts, dinghies and powerboats as they launched from the slipway. I helped once or twice to push boats out or haul them in, hoping for a tip.

Speke Hall and Farmers Fields

After the Boathouse was Speke Hall, a half-timbered Tudor house dating back to the 15th century. Its land then stretched to the Mersey shore. We used to enter via the shore and play in the grounds and woodland. We had a rope swing in the woods that we would use to swing across a gully that had a stream running to the river. The house was very ancient and it was supposed to be haunted. It had a moat around it into which the lady of the house had thrown her baby. It had a stone built bridge across the now dried out moat and carved in stone was the date 1645 and the stonemason's initials. We heard tales of priests who hid in the house in secret places that were called priest holes. These could be behind fireplaces, under the floor or in the roof. There was said to be a tunnel under the house to the river where they could escape and then row a boat across the river to freedom. No wonder we were a bit nervous by the house and to top it all the gardener would chase us if he found us in the gardens. We never got caught as the woods were thick and there were plenty of hiding places up in the trees or in the thick undergrowth on the ground.

Further up the coastal path we would come to the farmers' fields, these seemed to stretch for miles into the distance. We came up the path and across the fields to get to a pond where we would fish or just sit on the bank. The pond was called the "perchie" because of the perch fish in it and it was quite deep. The lads and sometimes the girls would swim in it. It was inhabited by "Ginny Green Teeth", who lived in the weeds, and she would snatch away unwary children. But more real and more frightening was the farmer who chased you off his land and I heard that occasionally he took pot shots with his shotgun. There were some people who stole his potatoes, carrots or cabbages as sometimes I passed them on the path with their bags full of produce.

Above: Aerial view of Speke Hall.

I loved to walk through the fields, especially the cornfields, as the smell was wonderful. The wild flowers nodding in the breeze, poppies like red flicked paint dotting the field and hedgerows, yellow oxe eye daisies, and blue cornflowers all mixed in with the corn.

As well as the beautiful flora there was a lot of wildlife. I jumped a mile when a pheasant flew up flapping and squawking when I disturbed it from its hideaway in the long grass. There were nests of harvest mice interwoven in the stalks of corn, weasels and stoats darting about the hedgerows and grey partridge, another bird that startled you by its whirring flight if you came too close.

Up above the seagulls squealing, lapwings pewitting, kestrels hovering, and for me the most glorious and beautiful sound in the world, the skylark. The majestic hovering in the sky, its trilling melodious song as it celebrated being alive. Even now when I hear the song of a skylark it takes me back to the glorious days up the shore, when life was carefree and simple.

Street Visitors

So I had this great contrast between the outdoor life and the enclosed life of the street. But even the street had lots going on to enliven the days. Some of the visitors brought a bit of colour and mystique to the street. The rag and bone men who announced their arrival with a very distinct call "any old iron, scrap iron, rags. "Any old iron" in a very nasal voice which you could hardly understand but knew immediately who it was. The knife grinder knocked on the door asking if you wanted knives, scissors or shears sharpened. I would watch fascinated as he ran the knives across the stone, the sparks flying until he had the edge he wanted. There was a man who came around on a bike with a box on the front, balloons trailing and comics for sale. The gypsies paid a visit; they looked like gypsies then, all dark hair and dripping jewellery. When they knocked on the door some people wouldn't answer but we always did. Mum was very superstitious and would buy some pegs or a lucky charm. I think this was because she was a bit worried that if you didn't buy you would be cursed. Other people visiting the street were the coal man, who was covered in coal dust, his face black.

He wore a heavy leather cover on his back to protect it as he heaved the bags of coal off the lorry on to his back to carry to the coalholes at the back of the house or under the stairs. I even heard some people stored it in the bath. Also black were the chimney sweeps who rode around on bikes with their brushes and sacks tied to the bike, sticking out like giant pipe cleaners.

Then there were the smartly dressed callers who were usually to be avoided as they were always after money. The insurance man or club man was one, he always amazed me because he would arrive like so many others, riding a bike, but what was different was that he only had one arm. I sometimes paid him and would give him the money and book. He would take them in his one hand and, somehow, mark the book with the amount, pocket the money and give you change.

The rent man or tallyman would come on Friday. I couldn't help hearing at times the conversations about the rent, to be exact, how to pay it. I answered the door to pork pie hat, the tallyman, and told him as I had been told to come back next week. He always got paid eventually; in fact I think we must have bought the house ten times over for we paid rent for 26 years.

Polio Scare

The house was without any modern amenities and was damp and cold. It was that damp, dad had trouble keeping the paper on the walls. I remember he nailed lino on the walls and papered over this to try to keep the paper dry. We only had a tin bath so having a bath was a problem especially now we were getting a bit bigger.

The miracle was we all stayed in pretty good health. Apart from my accidents and an operation on my sinus, I cannot remember being ill and I think that was true for all of us. We had the usual childhood illnesses, and caught head lice but nothing too serious.

I do remember one time when we thought we had a big problem, or more to the point, Patrick was ill. He stood at the top of the stairs one day, and his legs were paralysed so he just fell down the stairs when he tried to move. He was rushed to hospital with suspected polio. He was back home after a week but not before the house had been fumigated. I was totally ashamed because some of the lads skitted and treated us like lepers. There were a couple of lads in our school who had had polio, so next time they were giving sugar lumps out in the Methodist Church we would take them. These lumps were a vaccine and would stop us getting crippled.

A ritual we all went through was the nit comb. Just before bed mum would spread an 'Echo' out on the floor, put our heads over it and run the nit comb through our heads as everyone in our school had nits, it was an everlasting task. Every school got a visit from Nitty Nora, the nurse who checked your head for lice. The bad cases had their head shaved and purple medicine poured on their heads, so it was obvious who had the nits.

Changing Times; Some Good Some Bad

But times were changing. We now had a washing machine and a television set. It was only small and black and white, but better than the mahogany radio set or wireless as we called it with its luminous knobs and glowing tubes. We now had a gas poker to light the fire with. The whole area was now supposed to use smokeless fuel as we had been designated a smoke free area. As all the factories still poured out their smoke and fumes from giant chimneys, it seemed a waste of time. Some of the streets were now considered slums, and a giant clearance and demolition plan was put in place.

This had a catastrophic effect on the community and some feel it was never the same. Some of the streets knocked down were close knit communities and didn't take kindly to being moved to new housing estates like Kirby, Speke or Skelmersdale. I had friends in Sinclair Street, Shannon Street, and Thomas Street and these were knocked down. The pubs were left standing. They knocked a lot of King Street down including my Aunt Maud's shop where I used to go and get a penny drink for nothing. The pawnshop belonging to Frank Ketts was knocked down much to the dismay of his regular clients. I had a Chinese friend from school and their laundry was flattened. Grocery shops, betting shops all went – a sad sight. Missed most of all was the public urinal in the middle of King Street and Dale Street. The men used to play pitch and toss here, a gambling game and I used to keep "dixie", in other words if the police were on the way I would shout them and they would scatter, some of them into the gents. Most of the houses were condemned and did need to come down but one memorable building that should have stayed up was the Institute, a building something to do with the church. It was a fine Victorian Gothic building and gave a bit of grandeur and history to the area.

Above: Changing face of King Street.

The town planners flattened more houses than Hitler did in the last war. There were ugly scars everywhere. They did build on most of the land, more modern houses with amenities, unfortunately they never quite had the same community spirit as in the old streets and the flats they built in King Street ended up a total disaster.

Long Trousers and Dad's Razor

Time was racing now; everything was changing so fast including me. I was now playing around with my dad's razor, a lethal weapon if not used correctly and with my soft downy whiskers, I often nicked my throat.

The summer soon ended and we were getting ready to return to school. My brother Patrick would be joining me in the senior school.

One thing I remember on my return, I still had short trousers on and a lot of my class mates had long trousers, but to be honest I loved short pants and dreaded the day I would wear long trousers. I always liked the fresh air on my legs and as I was a footballer I had brown well-muscled legs.

Football now was the be all of everything. There was a song out about then called "Football Crazy", that was me.

My ambition to be a footballer was "pie in the sky" some people said, but others said I had the ability if I just kept dedicated. I was dedicated, spending every spare hour perfecting my skills, often on my own, until it went dark, sometimes later, under the street lamps. I would juggle the ball for hours, practise trapping the ball, swerving and driving it. I would do everything except eat the ball, but I did sleep with it.

Above: Playing in Senior Team with Everton Shield. I was only 13!

On reflection maybe I spent too much time on my own as football was a team game. I tended to be greedy and keep the ball to myself when playing, dribbling everyone in sight, and the other lads got fed up and would say "pass it, you're too greedy", or call me fancy pants for doing too many tricks.

School was the only outlet at this time for representative football, and we all took great pride in our school team.

We had some good players so the team was very successful. I wanted to play for Liverpool Boys as there were a couple of local lads who had played for them and gone on to play for Liverpool F.C. or Everton F.C. Some of the lads and myself were chosen for trials for Liverpool Boys. They had two teams, an under 14 and an under 15 team and we were trying for the Under 14s.

The trials were at Penny Lane or Grove Mount to give the ground its proper title. There were hundreds of boys for trial and we played lots of games. After every match there was a process of elimination, with your name being called out for further trials if you were successful. I had my name called out a few times and made the final trials but I didn't make the final squad and was bitterly disappointed at the time. I consoled myself by thinking that I was probably too small because at that time it was said that Liverpool Boys liked big lads. Whatever the reason I was determined to get in the Under 15 team the next year and so I set a target of training harder to improve skills and to grow bigger.

I was told to hang from the washing line with weights on my feet to stretch myself. I didn't do this but I did do lots of stretching exercises and I also ate everything put in front of me.

At home we weren't starved but I always felt hungry and would eat my own meals and finish off any one else's if they left any scraps. I had such a healthy appetite because I was never still and burned it all off and I was now starting to sprout and grow out of my clothes, much to my mothers dismay.

Unlike a lot of boys at school I liked school meals. We had a nice canteen with plenty to eat. To get a meal you needed a ticket and we stood in line to buy these, or if you qualified you could get them free. I did qualify, coming from a large family but I remember I had to overcome my dad's reluctance to what he called charity handouts. My mum told him it was our right as he worked and paid taxes, and anyway "our Michael needs all the food he can get".

If you were having a free dinner you got a red ticket, if you paid it was a green one. This was an unnecessary discrimination that I always remember as being unfair as some lads would skit your red meal ticket. This didn't stop me eating it all up and occasionally we got "seconds" and I would go up and get a second helping of cheese pie, mince and potatoes or fish. Whatever it was I would eat it, even the dreaded semolina pudding was eaten with relish.

Although I was distracted in school by football and now girls had started to look better, I still maintained a decent level of achievement in my schoolwork. If I found something interesting I would listen and study, if not I switched off and struggled. I struggled at Maths but did well in History, Geography, Social Studies and Religious Studies. In fact, in my third year I came top of the class in History and near the top in Religious Studies, but near the bottom in Maths.

Innocence Lost

The age of innocence was over. I became aware that the world was a dangerous place. I was terrified listening to the television. I heard the President of America tell us of the threat of Russia, more to the point, the nuclear arms of Russia on the way to Cuba, an island very close to America. I couldn't sleep for days and was convinced the world was at an end. This threat retreated when Russia recalled their ships and nuclear weapons. Another shock was the killing of President Kennedy by a lone assassin in Dallas. The world was shocked and everyone still says they can remember the exact moment and where they were when the President was killed. I can't but it was another reminder of the danger in the world.

These images were all seen on our small black and white television from Radio Rentals. Talking about black and white, I first became aware of racism about that time, especially in America with the Civil Rights Movement and Martin Luther King. He was a great speaker and he made an impression on me as he led marches and had his dreams.

I cannot remember seeing a black face until senior school. I noticed when we played a school called Granby Street at football, most of the team was black which was a new experience for us. I always had a natural curiosity about people, their background and culture, I already had in me the seeds of a radical. I started questioning, why some people were very rich and others poor? Why some people had baths and nice houses and others not? Why did we have wars? Why there was racism? At that time I kept most of these thoughts to myself because no one else seemed to care. Anyway, football still came first and my ambition to sign for a football club.

Tizer the Appetizer

The school holidays were upon us again, another term had ended. I had made progress in my education and in my football, representing the school for my age group, and the age group above me. At the age of 13 going on fourteen, a year makes a lot of difference, and when I played for the year above me I was dwarfed by the other lads, but I suppose my skill carried me through.

I had two targets for the school holidays, to build myself up and learn to swim. As circumstances unravelled, I had plenty of opportunity to do both.

My father now worked for "Tizer" of "Tizer the Appetizer" fame, a soft drink company. He was a driver/salesman. The job entailed driving his lorry full of orange, tizer, lemonade, dandelion and burdock and cola drinks to the hundreds of shops he delivered to in Liverpool. He took the order, delivered the full bottles and came out with the empties. This was a hard job physically, as the crates of pop were very heavy. It was also mentally demanding as he worked out the cost of the order, wrote it down, took the money and gave change. Another problem in some areas was the stealing of bottles off the back of the lorry. Unlike some pop company's he had no second man and that's where I came in. I was cheap and available and didn't cost too much to feed. I was to stack the empty crates on the back of the lorry and keep guard at the same time.

"Pat, Pat, Pat", that was my mother shouting dad to get up. She always had to repeat herself until he got up. I was up first and ready for the day. I cannot remember which mode of transport we had at the time because over the years dad had so many. Firstly, I remember the motorbike, then he attached a sidecar, and then for some reason he had been reduced to a pushbike, but then came the crème-de-la-crème, an impressive Wolsley car. This was an ex police car, with silver steel bumpers and an impressive badge. At that time not many people had cars and for a large family like ours, it was a great surprise to our neighbours.

Now that our family was complete, 7 children and two adults, if we were to have a car it needed to be big and we all fitted into this one. I can still remember the smell and the cool touch of the leather and straps that you could hold on to at the side, feeling like royalty.

So off we went to work, dad would drop me off somewhere near the depot, usually Sefton Park which was near the depot in Aigburth Vale. Dad was not allowed a second man, certainly not a schoolboy, hence the secrecy. All the drivers used helpers but none as young as me. We would start the day with tea and toast in a café, then off on our rounds.

The round we had stretched for miles across Liverpool. In those days there were still thousands of small corner shops, and these were the shops we called at to deliver pop. The problem was that dad seemed to have all the areas that were known as tough areas. He had shops along the docks of Kirkdale and Bootle, the famous Scotland Road, Vauxhall Road, parts of Anfield, Dingle and the city centre. I loved working on the lorry, you met some characters and the shopkeepers were friendly giving me sweets or cakes. There was the odd miserable one but most people I met were good to me. I was soon building my muscles up with all the hard work lifting and stacking crates. I got a bit cocky though and when some young lads started taunting me and trying to steal Tizer bottles, I got off the lorry to chase them, a big mistake. Dad was in the shop and had told me never to get off the lorry, just shout him if anyone was stealing. I should have done what I was told and I got battered for my stupidity. The lads jumped on me, I smacked a couple but soon I was overwhelmed and got a kicking. I shouted out and dad came, after what seemed an age, and he saved me but told me off for disobeying him. In the hot weather of summer we sold loads of pop sometimes selling a whole wagon full. All the shops would be buying and even people on the street trying to buy some, one perk of the job was we could have a drink any time we wanted. I loved the "Jusoda" pop and drank it out of the bottle, this was a bit "dodgy" as once dad swallowed a wasp that had fallen in the open bottle and it stung him in the throat.

Dinner we usually had in Frank's café on the Dock Road, as he was one of dad's customers. I loved the sausage on toast, or a meat pie and chips, or egg, beans and chips. The smells were lovely. The Dock Road had a smell of its own, very sweet and pungent. They were the smells of molasses or grain ships as they filled the warehouses that lined the road.

Garston Baths and Youth Club

I was now growing and getting muscles, fulfilling my ambition to get fitter and stronger for the football. The other part of my plan was to learn to swim. Most of my mates could swim but I was proud, a big fault, as I was determined to learn on my own.

After a hard day on the wagon I would get a couple of bob, enough to get in the baths and get some chips for tea.

The public baths was an old Victorian building, built of brick and sandstone with miles of tiling inside. I had been before but only splashed around the shallow end and that was only 3 feet, the deep end was 6 feet. There were two pools, one small and the other was called the big pool. The big pool had lockers right around the pool, one side for boys and the other side for girls. It had a skylight running the length of the pool. The complex also had slipper baths. They were ordinary bathrooms for the people who didn't have one at home at the time of building, in fact some families still don't have a bathroom. Attached to the baths was the wash house, where a lot of women congregated to do their washing, drying and ironing.

Above: Bank Field House trip to football tournament in Boston.

I paid my money and went in. The noise was electric, a maelstrom of echoes and cries and screams, there was a very moist atmosphere like a hothouse, water splashing everywhere across the tiled floor, and condensation on the walls and skylights.

I slipped into the water in the shallow end hoping none of my mates were in. I held the bar and kicked my legs and then let go and tried to float. I sank but kept kicking until I floated, then I thrashed my arms and legs around, swallowed loads of water, but eventually I swam a couple of strokes. I was over the moon. I went every night for weeks until I could swim a breadth. I was thrilled. At last I could swim. It was like when I first rode a bike. I felt a great sense of achievement.

Above: Brian Taylor training Bank Field House boys in athletics.

It may have seemed unusual to learn to swim this way but we never went with the school in all the years I had attended junior or senior school. I was too proud to ask my friends to teach me, and my dad, who had taken me once when I was very young, never had the time.

I learned to ride a bike the same way, even driving a car later in life was the same, on my own, breaking the law, all because of false pride. I learnt later in life the folly of my ways and realised everyone has to learn and there was no failure if you tried.

Life outside of school was starting to broaden. I started to attend the local youth club. This seemed to be just an extension and grown up version of the play centre.

The main reason I went to the club at "Bankfield House" was for the football and athletics. They had a floodlit five a side court. They also had table tennis, snooker, music, and dances, trips out, walks and girls.

Bankfield House was a church youth club and was paid for by the people of Garston who had donated money and bought individual bricks for years.

This is where it all happened. Where boy met girl – boys tested each other out like rutting stags. Dances were held, there was an art club, folk singing, football, netball or just hanging about creating impressions, which was so important if you were a mod or a rocker.

It was hard trying to be grown up. What should I say? What shall I wear? What should I do? How shall I walk? Who should be my friends? The worries were endless, especially as we were trying to grow up too quickly.

Really though, I didn't have a lot of choices. Even if I wanted them as I had no money to buy clothes. I was the eldest of seven and there wasn't enough money to go round after paying for essentials. How could I try and be sophisticated, we never even had a bathroom. I was fourteen. I had never ever used a phone, in fact, I didn't even know anyone who had one. I slept in a room with four other lads; I had never been out of Liverpool, spending most of my time within the sight of the gas tanks. I didn't know if I should have long or short hair. Hair had started to get longer with the Beatles and Rolling Stones. Dad called them longhaired louts and school frowned upon long hair. A lot of school friends were sent home to get a hair cut. Haircuts in our home started to cause problems. For years dad had cut our hair. You could have any style you wanted as long as it was a crew cut. Dad had a pair of clippers that he ruthlessly ran over our heads, shaving the lot off. This was great when we were kids, but now we wanted it a bit longer, especially my brother Patrick, who screamed and shouted and ran away because he wanted long hair. Eventually dad relented a bit and let our hair grow. He even let us go to the barbers in the lane. There you could get a choice of haircut plus a penny sweet, but you had to pay. That was the problem.

There was a barber in the family, Uncle Ernie, and his son, but their shop was down Park Road in the Dingle and was too far to go.

Street Corners

Every street had a corner shop, then, or so it seemed, they were the mainstays of the community. You could buy anything at these shops, from bread to milk to sweets, cakes, biscuits, cigarettes, plasters, nuts, fire lighters, paraffin, tins of beans, safety pins and drawing pins. In one shop you could buy penny sweets. The shopkeeper would have the sweets on a tray and you picked what you wanted as he held out the tray.

Women would use the corner shop to catch up on the news and gossip, just like the men used the pubs. If you were hard up you could get most things "on the slate" and once or twice I would go to the shop and say "me mam will see you tomorrow", and as "me mam" was a good payer we always got tick. In those days you had shops for everything. I remember in Window Lane, our main shopping street, there was a butcher, grocer, fish shop, cake shop, newsagents, cobbler, wool shop, chip shop, a barbers, haberdashery, clothes shop, dry cleaners, dairy, hardware, the list was endless.

Career Choices

I was now coming to the last year of my time in school. A time to celebrate because at the time you could leave school at 15 years of age and get a job, earn money and be grown up. Now I realise it was far too early to leave, a few stayed on, the ones who realised the value of education. Although I didn't try as hard as I should have, I sat the school leaving exam and passed in six subjects.

My overriding ambition was still to play professional football and most of my time was taken up with this dream. All my training, swimming, and working with dad had made me stronger but not much bigger in height.

Unlike today a young footballer would be spotted at an early age, guided and brought on gently. The only chance of being spotted would be through schoolboy football and this meant Liverpool Boys, so this was still my goal. To represent the city at football meant you were one of the potential stars of the future.

The time was fast approaching to make decisions as to the future. The school had arranged for a careers officer to come in and give us some advice. When my turn for interview came, I went in, sat down and answered her question: "and what is it you would like to do?" When I answered "footballer", she replied "don't be stupid", get serious. I then told a lie and said "bricklayer". Right she said, you can go to Riversdale College and if you pass the exam you can study for building skills. The exam would entail English and Maths and I would have to study hard. I had a nice teacher for my last year, a Mr. Collinson, a very gentle man whose worst punishment was to make you stand in the corner, this I did often, still playing to the crowd. Occasionally, to his regret he would send me for the cane. A Mr Galia handed out the cane and he seemed to relish this task, but as ever I was determined not to cry and I didn't, even though the pain was excruciating.

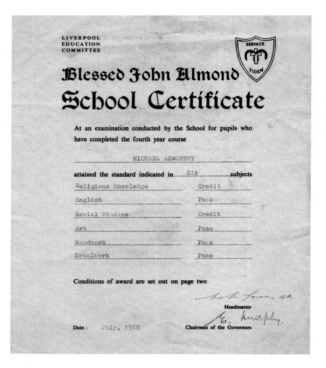

LIVERPOOL
EDUCATION
COMMITTEE

Blessed John Almond

School Certificate

At an examination conducted by the School for pupils who have completed the fourth year course

MICHAEL AXWORTHY

attained the standard indicated in _____Six_____ subjects

Religious Knowledge	Credit
English	Pass
Social Studies	Credit
Art	Pass
Woodwork	Pass
Metalwork	Pass

Conditions of award are set out on page two

Headmaster

Date: July, 1968

Chairman of the Governors

I was learning in school, but not a lot. I can't remember doing my homework. I think the idea was to furnish us with the basic secondary education to equip us for the world we would be expected to go into: the world of factories, offices and docks. Not for us the rarefied atmosphere of higher education. To be fair, there were one or two exceptions, but for the majority, we had to set our sights low.

Rebellion And Music

Man had flown in space, or to be more precise, Yuri Gagarin the Russian Cosmonaut, had. We now had transistor radios and computers were getting smaller and were now the size of a fridge! The Beatles were conquering America but we still didn't have a bath!

We did however, have a very old record player bought from a second hand shop, or was it a jumble sale? I'm not sure, as we got quite a few things second hand, including my brother Dan's violin, and a piano for Peter. Peter was one of the twins and incidentally they both grew up to be very good players. On one trip to a jumble sale with my mum we came home with hundreds of old seventy-eight records and pictures to hang on the walls. In no way did I feel poor or embarrassed by our jumble sale trips; in fact I enjoyed them. I loved to search and sort through the different tables of goods piled high with clothes, knickknacks, records and books, a veritable treasure trove of booty. The quality of the goods depended upon where the sale was held. The richer the area, the better the quality and consequently the best sale was in the leafy suburbs of Allerton, at the Jewish Synagogue's nearly new sale. I might not have had a school uniform jacket but for my last six months at school I had a smart woollen checked jacket from the Synagogue.

I used to sit with a girl on the step in our street wearing the same jacket and listening to records, talking and feeling strange, very strong urges. I asked her if I could borrow her Beatle records and she said yes, so I took them down the street and played them on our crackly jumble sale record player. Then I would pick up Dad's guitar to copy the Beatles. It wasn't long before the bashing of the chords snapped a string or two. Dad went mad and asked why I didn't play properly and gently. He was right but this was hard to do when you wanted to be a pop star.

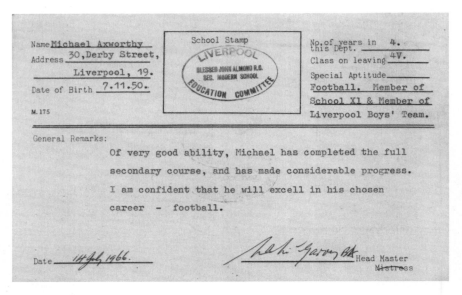

I didn't really want to be a pop star. I still wanted to be a footballer, as my testimonial from school shows, and to this end I was still striving. If I had put as much effort into my schoolwork, I would have been a genius and gone to University. But this wouldn't have been an option anyway, I was the eldest of seven and no way could I be supported through higher education. I didn't aspire to that ambition, in all the years I went to school I never did any homework, I wasn't even asked or pushed to do any and to be honest at the time I preferred football and games after school.

Family Members

I was very much wrapped up in myself. I had five brothers and one sister and I never took much interest in them. I think it was every man for himself but to give some insight into what happened in the family here is an inventory.

Dad sang a lot and acted as a concert secretary in our local church club. He was a mechanical wizard, doing all his own repairs on his car, motorbike or push bike. He even built a sidecar to attach to his motorbike. Dad was always making or repairing something.

Mum was a lady, had great looks as well as being a hardworking mother and loyal wife – not in vogue these days but what greater gift can you give to seven children, than love. She was a good dancer and when we grew up she enjoyed a night out with dad. A good dance, a game of bingo, a couple of drinks and she was in heaven.

Above: Now we are seven.

Patrick, next born after me was a loveable rogue, always up to something. He joined the sea cadets and had a lovely uniform in which he dressed proudly for a photograph. His other interests were bird watching, firing his catapult and smoking. We had the odd boxing match but nothing too serious.

Tim was the third born and unlike me had dark hair, he was good at school and he even passed the Eleven Plus, to cap it all he was good at sport. I don't know if he was very pious but the priest asked mum and dad if he could go to a seminary with a view to becoming a priest? This request was turned down flat.

Keith, the fourth born was quiet until he was upset and then all hell broke loose, and his older brothers upset him a lot. He also was good at sport, especially football and he could have been brilliant but too often he was sent off the field for his fiery temper. At other times butter wouldn't melt in his mouth and he was well liked.

Daniel was the fifth born, blonde and as strong as an ox. He took part in bodybuilding as a kid and was known for his muscles and strength. Unusually he bought a violin from a second hand shop, had private lessons and mastered the instrument. He became a great player.

Peter was the Sixth Son, but as mum's first born a son Francis unfortunately died, Peter was the 'seventh son of a seventh son' and in Irish legend this meant he would be exceptional. Well he could spin a tale and dream for England, but he had great musical talent, sang opera and learned to play the piano and was a great entertainer.

Angela, our only sister was the seventh born and a bit of a tomboy but was a beautiful girl, became Miss Garston and also modelled and had her picture in the papers.

As you can see there was a lot going on in Derby Street with my siblings, most of this was in the future but I missed a lot of it. I suppose I was totally engrossed in myself, like the earth thinking all the planets revolved around him only to discover on growing up, that he was just a small part of our galaxy going around the sun.

Bricklaying or Football

I was coming up to my last six months in school, with still no real idea what I would do on leaving. I had stated an interest in a course at the local technical college in bricklaying and building. No real idea why, I just had a vague notion of wanting a skilled trade. My main idea was still to play football, but how?

We had a good school team and beat all comers on our route to the league and cup double. Fate took a hand here, for the cup final was to be held at Penny Lane, the home of the Liverpool Boys team and the manager of Olive Mount, the team we were playing, was also manager of the Liverpool Boys.

There was a lot of excitement in the school about the forthcoming match and I remember the music teacher teaching the school a song for the final. It was a sort of battle cry. This made the players feel very important and we knew it was down to us to bring honour to the school.

Everything came together for this game. All the training and the practice paid off. I had one of those games you dream of. Every pass went to feet, every tackle made, two goals scored and the team won 6-0, a great result in the cup final. I felt six feet tall with all the cheering and congratulations, and to top it all, Tom Saunders, the manager of Liverpool Boys told our teacher that I was to report for training for the Boys team the following week. I was in heaven.

Wearing the Liver Bird

All I had dreamed about now seemed so close. I reported for training the following week and met the boys who had been playing for the team for a year, some of them already committed to professional clubs when they left school.

Then a dream came true. Tom Saunders told me I would be playing against Birkenhead in the Dimmer Cup Final, quite an honour. I didn't have time to think. Everything was happening so quickly, the game was the next day.

I told everyone I could, I was so proud and honoured and nervous about my debut.

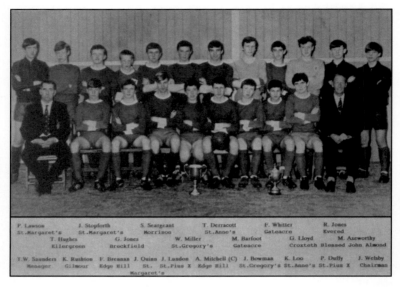

Above: Liverpool boys football team 1965.

When I pulled on the red shirt with the Liver Bird on my chest, I had never felt so proud. As I ran out on to the pitch it felt as if all the years of training had finally paid off and come together in this moment.

I had a good game and felt confident. I enjoyed the crowds' applause and we won the game 4-1.

Unknown to me there were some relatives and teachers from school and also my dad and scouts from professional clubs.

The next day it was in the Echo. I had made my debut and had a good game. I was to play in the next game against Ellesmere Port. The teachers in school congratulated me and fellow pupils were impressed. After all the years of training and dreaming I felt I had made it.

We drew the next game against Ellesmere Port. It was a quick end to end game, not a lot of skill, a typical school game. My next game was against a Greater Manchester area team called Middleton, which ended in a draw. I was presented with my Liverpool Schools badge after the game, I was so proud when I went into school the next day with the badge on my chest.

Dreams and Disappointments

The weekend arrived and on the Saturday evening a knock came at the door. It was a little man called Joe Armstrong, a scout for Manchester United. The next hour was a blur, all I remember was he asked me if I wanted to train with the great Man-United? I had trained all my life for this and so I said yes right away. I was told to await his instructions in the next few days. I couldn't sleep with all the excitement of Man-United the great "Busby Babes" also George Best, Bobby Charlton and Dennis Law. What a team! What a dream!

It may seem strange now but there was no animosity between Manchester United and Liverpool, unlike now, yes there was rivalry but friendly. I was also visited by a Liverpool scout Tom Bush, and asked to train with them, I made a decision to try United first, which on reflection was a mistake, but I was only a kid then.

Eventually the day came for me to go to Manchester. I travelled by train and taxi to The Cliff the training ground of United.

So there I was at last, on the field with famous professional footballers, a dream come true. I looked anything but a footballer. I was so skinny, had buck teeth and was terrified but I had one saving grace, I had great skill as a footballer and felt totally at home with a ball at my feet. The next few months are a blur now but I remember some very significant moments.

I remember being taken to Old Trafford and meeting the great Matt Busby, his voice so soft and reassuring. He then chatted and showed me around and coming towards us down the corridor to the dressing rooms, was the legendary Bobby Charlton. He shook my hand, I mumbled something, hoping I looked like a footballer and sounding grown up.

Above: Playing at Penny Lane for Liverpool Boys.

I wanted to blurt out "Where do I sign? Will I get paid?" I came out of the tunnel, looked at the pitch and imagined the great goals I would score in the next few years. I cannot remember chronological dates, just some of the memorable events. One day stands out! Brian Kidd was a well-respected junior player and he seemed to have been allocated to look after my welfare.

After one training session he took me home to his house for dinner. He lived quite local as he was from Manchester. He was a great lad and his family were very warm. Brian's mum made a lovely dinner and I remember there was a few laughs about my Liverpool accent. Later that evening we went to Old Trafford to watch Manchester United versus Panathaniakos, the Greek Champions, in the European Cup. United won and as I watched I saw myself scoring a hat-trick and dreamt of glory for myself and my family. There was magic in watching a game under floodlights and being one of a big crowd.

I was in digs for a short time and I found this hard to adjust to. Eventually I went to a house with four other junior players and felt more at home. I made friends with a Welsh lad with an Irish name, Peter O'Sullivan, also with an Englishman with an Italian name Carlo Sartori, and also with a Scotsman with an Irish name John Fitzpatrick.

Another Red Shirt

My first game in the famous red shirt and black socks was against Bury, not a particularly great game to start with but one I would have to play well in if I was to be taken on as a player. It was hard to shine in these games. It seemed a hundred miles an hour and very physical. For a skinny boy like me this was not much of a stage to show my skills, even though I was a tough lad from Liverpool who would not be bullied. I nearly scored, showed flashes of my skill and felt quite proud to represent Manchester United. I asked the trainer why we wore black socks. He told me it was to remember the tragedy of Munich, when a plane carrying the Manchester United team and reporters, crashed on the way back from a European football game. This crash resulted in the death of some great young players and also of some well-known press people. The crash at Munich happened in 1958 when Manchester where trying to be the first British team to win the European Cup. They would realise this ambition in 1967 with my friend Brian Kidd who was only 18 at the time. The win was great for English football, for Matt Busby the Manager who had been seriously hurt at Munich but most of all it was a victory in memory of the great team that had been decimated by the tragedy.

Any game between Manchester City and Manchester United was a keenly fought game, even if it was only the junior teams. I played in this fixture in one of my first games, wearing a United shirt. I remember one part of the game when I scored an equalising goal in the first half with a good left foot drive. I never scored many with my left foot so I was pleased. We won the game 4-2 and Joe Armstrong congratulated me on my goal. I felt I was on my way with United, but still not sure of my future status.

Joe Armstrong, the chief scout, approached me after training one day and told me I had done well and United wanted to sign me as a amateur player and he would get me a job to earn some money.

From Old Trafford Back to Garston

Anyway, I was still trying to impress and wanted to eventually become a professional, so I stayed a season. I remember one game we had against Bolton Wanderers. I don't know how much time had gone when I chased a through ball, intending to beat the goalkeeper to the ball and slip it past him into the net. Unfortunately, we collided and I was knocked out and being a tough lad, I had never suffered an injury before. I think his knee caught me on the head and I had concussion. The next fuzzy memory is of the trainer holding up fingers for me to count. After concussion you cannot play on. This was a precaution in case of further injury. I must have caused the trainer some concern as he decided to take me to Old Trafford to see the club doctor and to receive some treatment.

Old Trafford was a few miles away so I came around a bit. It was unfortunate circumstances but what a thrill. The first team of stars was playing at home; I heard the crowd first then saw the ground. We went in a side entrance and soon we were in the dressing room. I was told to lie on the treatment table in the middle of the dressing room. I waited a bit and then a doctor came. He looked into my eyes, made a decision that I did not have to go to the hospital, but that it would be better if I was taken home in a car all the way back to Liverpool. Then a moment I will never forget happened. The whistle had blown in the big match and in the players came, surprised to see a young kid on the treatment table. I looked around in awe. Here were the great players I hoped to emulate. There was George Best, Dennis Law, Bobby Charlton and all the rest of the team. They were kind to me, making jokes and rubbing my head. It was like a dream but I know it happened. John Ashton, the trainer who had taken me to Old Trafford said he would take me home, but his son John Junior said he would take me. John Junior was now in the first team and was in the dressing room. I remember a year later watching him play in the European Cup Final for Manchester United, along with the other players I have mentioned. They fulfilled Matt Busby's dream of winning the European Cup.

I was eventually driven all the way back to Liverpool by John Ashton Senior, a gentleman if ever there was one. There were no motorways then and I didn't know the way, but I remember saying, "just aim for the airport". This he did and from there I knew my way home.

I was wondering what John Ashton would think of Garston, especially "Under the Bridge" dominated by the gastank which next to the Airport, was a landmark.

Anyway, we found our house and went in. Dad and Mum were surprised and a little tongue tied, but they needn't have worried, as John was a perfect gentleman and down to earth. I had already left the boarding house in Manchester and was living at home, and John Aston said to my parents, I needed feeding up! Which surprised them both as I never stopped eating.

After a season I was still an amateur player with no job, and was not offered professional terms, so I was out one night with my friends and one said, "Do you want a job". Well I needed money so I said yes and before I knew it I was working. Now my childhood was behind me and a lot of experiences in front of me,including more football wearing blue shirts and red shirts and many different jobs, buts that is a long story, and a story for the future.

Above: Home again.

Between the Gasworks and the Church

In Blank Verse

Like all adults I often dream of happy childhood days,
a thought can take me back to the street I grew up in
a small terraced house in Derby street under the bridge.

The street I grew up in has long since been demolished
but memories live on in my mind and in old photographs
I felt I needed to write down and share these memories.

The following words and old photographs attempt this.
The work is not meant to be a complete historic record,
more a fond remembrance of a community as it was then.

I decided to write these childhood memories as blank verse
each line trying to paint a picture of a precious memory.
This is how I perceived it when growing up and in my dreams.

I would like to thank the Garston Historical Society and
John Booth for the use of some old photographs.
John was our old next-door neighbour in Derby Street.

All pictures are in black and white
I believe black and white best illustrates this era
A time before the world went colour.

Under the Bridge

A maze of streets built of brick and grassless
Sandwiched between the docks and the railway
Dominated by gasometers soaring black and high
In their dark shadow St. Michael's ancient church
With its clock tower ringing bell and graveyard
Spanning Church Road a brick and iron bridge
The entrance to "under the bridge" community
A hive of industry then working day and night

Above: Under the Bridge, Garston 1960.

Industry

The Gasworks – the Match Works – Garston Docks
The Railways – the Bobbin Works and Blackwell's
The Tannery – the Timber Yards the Mirror Works
Buzzers – klaxons and sirens called people to work
Streets busy as men and women rise for the day
Dressing – praying – laughing and eating in the rush
Crowds marching quickly to their places of work
Flat caps – scarves – and boots of the stevedores
Chimneys belching smoke the air thick with smog
Steam trains huffing and puffing over the bridge
Factories manufacturing goods for all the world
The Bottle Works smelting glass for sorted bottles
The Mirror Works made moulded frames for pictures
Bryant & May splitting logs for red tipped matches
The Tannery turning raw cow hides into sole leather
The Gasworks turning coal into gas and coke heaps
The scream of the Saw Mills blows sawdust airborne

*Above: A view of Garston's skyline from Speke Road Bridge, showing
Garston Parish Church, Railways, Docks and the river.*

Above: Garston Docks in the 1960s.

Garston Docks

Giant cranes swinging loads on the river sky line
Lifting timber and steel from giant berthed ships
Ships from exotic climes bringing yellow bananas
Coal ships were fully loaded for export overseas
We collected coal that washed up on the foreshore
From the dock wall I looked down on the deep water
Watching the ships entering and leaving the docks
And watching the dockers working hard on the ships
They hooked up chains for the cranes to lift above
They hand balled timber into slings to be unloaded
The main tools were a docker's hook and raw muscle
I watched cargo as it was lifted out of the ships hold
And watched the sun reflected on the still deep water
In the distance clouds scudded across the Welsh hills

Schools

Children dressed quickly in the cold mornings
Then walked to school with their best friends
Three schools for all the different traditions
Holy Trinity R.C., Banks Road C.P., St. Michael's C.E.
All the children lived and played together
The classrooms tasted of dusty white chalk

Above: Holy Trinity School and Church.

The residue from squeaky chalk on blackboards
Fingers stained blue from leaking ink wells
Name scratched desks and hard wooden seats
Iron discipline dished out by cruel swishing canes
Morning assembly tuneless hymns and prayers
Damp cloakrooms and disinfected outside toilets
Penny biscuits at break and cold school milk
Hot school dinners free for the poorer children
Lessons the three r's reading writing arithmetic
The times table chanted to a steady clapped rhythm
Football and fighting in the school playground

Stood in a straight line when the whistle went
Making friends and avoiding the school bullies
Liking some teachers scared by the headmaster
Children were sick caretaker brought sawdust
We had a football eleven and a cricket team
Minutes and hours then days turning to years
Best days of your life but not believing adults
Silver streaked sleeves and baggy short pants
Shoes scuffed with soles that flapped loosely
Scraped scabby knees and bumps on your head
Bell went at four o'clock then all home to play

*Above: Holy Trinity School Cricket Team completing the double - Liverpool Under 11
Cricket and Football Champions 1962.*

Street Games and Celebrations

Into the street the centre of all our lives
Children – playing – laughing – skipping –running
Street games hopscotch on square flagstones
Glass marbles rolled into cracked pavements
Billy – kick-the-can – hide and seek and hand tick
Skipping ropes-singing rhymes and hoola hoops
Football and cricket wickets getting told off
For chalking goal posts on the gable end walls
Lamp posts were climbed and we swung on ropes
Childhood squabbles, fisticuffs, bruises and tears
Mothers consoling drying eyes making you better
On Coronation Day the street had a big celebration
Tables were put out in the street laden with food
The street was decorated with bunting and flags

Above and opposite: Derby Street at Coronation time.
Our house in the background.

A pageant was held and a king and queen chosen
The local scout group marched down the streets
Playing tuneless bugles and banging the big bass drums
Celebrations went on into the night then bedtime
Once a year we decorated a lorry for the Carnival
We entered as emergency ward ten on one occasion
All the children swathed in bandages and red lipstick
One summer we all went to Southport on a Charabanc
We also went to Banks Road School for playcentre
Games and play were held after school for all children
We played table tennis hitting the ball with wooden bats
We threw beanbags and played billiards with tipless cues
Played football or drew pictures with crayons or danced

The Street the House and Corner Shop

We had a front parlour the best room in the house
Smelling of polish- chintz curtains and Steinway piano
Also a long lobby with an electric meter cubby-hole
We eat and sat and played in the small living room
At the rear the small back kitchen and stone sink
Up the stairs a landing and off it two big bedrooms
Also a tiny box bedroom at the back of the house
Lino covered the floors or tiles in the back kitchen
And placed around the house different sized mats
The front door was always open to our neighbours
Neighbours stood on the steps laughing and chatting
Steps were cleaned and brushed then stone whitened
Women wore headscarves with rollers underneath
And also flowery patterned pinnies with big pockets
Prams were pushed to the shops and the wash house
Not far to walk Kettlewell's the busy corner shop
Fresh bread – margarine – best butter if you're lucky
Biscuits – steri milk – cigarettes and broken biscuits
A bag of sugar – strawberry jam and matches on tick
Wooden counters – ringing tills – sweets in glass jars
I also went to Aunt Maude's shop in King Street
She would give me cinder toffee and a penny drink

Above: Shops in King Street.

Left: My Dad's old Wolsley Police car, rear view.

Right: Derby Street, with the gas Tank clearly visible at the top of our street.

Above: Front view of the Wolsley, just been polished.

The coal man dirty faced with leather back padding
Strong arms lifted lumpy heavy sacks off the wagon
Carried on their backs then emptied into coal holes
And Mr Joy had a horse pulling his rattling milk float
Delivering the milk the horse clopping up the street
A neighbour collected any manure for his allotment
Five o'clock buzzer goes and workers return home
To coal fires – noisy children and hot steaming stew
Washing away the grime and sweat in our tin bath
Hanging on the wall rusting away in the back yard
Down the whitewashed yard to the outside toilet
With its wooden seat and ripped newspaper to use
Little squares crumbled up hanging on a rusty nail
The cistern froze during the big freeze of winters.

Bath Time and Supper

Children called in as the dark nights draw in
To be washed – tar covered knees were scrubbed
In the tin bath placed in front of a blazing fire
Then our hair cut by Dad with his own clippers
No television we listened to a wet battery radio
Or listened to stories about our family histories
Or family played music and joined in a singsong
For supper enjoyed a hot piece of buttered toast
Or a jam butty or if naughty went to bed hungry

Bedtime

Sleeping under blankets and coats top to tail
Too hot in the summer freezing in bad winters
No central heating frost laced the windows
Smoking breath steaming in the chilly cold air
We were very rarely ill or visited the doctors
Folk medicine was still practised in most homes
From birth to death women helped when needed
Mustard baths and poultices helped heal colds
Sweaty socks tied round necks eased sore throats
Hot toddies for coughs and bicarbonate for stings
Dock leaves for nettle stings and salt for warts
A chamber pot saves a trip down the dark yard
A single light bulb switched off then darkness
From downstairs shouts to go to sleep or else
In later years growing up we slept in bunk beds

Breakfast & Washing Day in Kitchen

Early to rise as workers pass under our window
For breakfast porridge with milk, salt and sugar
No waste or choice all ate up or go out hungry
We had a quick swill under the single cold tap
Or used the hot water geyser for boiling water
Our house had no luxury of a washing machine
Mother washed clothes by hand in a dolly tub
Using a washboard fairy soap and elbow grease
All squeezed through the wheels of Mum's mangle
Then pegged out to dry in the sun on a washing line
If it rained washing hung inside on a pulley maiden
The washing dripped on you if you sat underneath
Dirty nappies put in soak before they were washed
All hung out proudly white squares and gleaming
A blanket was spread on the table to do the ironing
With a flat iron which had been warmed on the fire

Wash House and the Baths

The wash house and baths were in the Village Centre
Large bed sheets were taken to the local wash house
Piled high on a rickety pram
pushed down Banks Road
Wash house steaming
smelling of soapy cleanliness
It had washing machines
dryers and women ironing
All noise and bubbles – wet
floors and idle gossiping

Public Baths

Showers to wash your dirty feet before jumping in
Chlorine stinging the eyes skin going crinkly
Girls with rubber caps and children have arm bands
Shallow end for learners deep end for swimmers
Children's screams echoed around the tiled walls
Blue water shimmered reflecting the skylights
Cubicles with wooden doors surround the pool
Lifeguards with whistles and long barge poles
Baggy woolly costumes fell around our knees
Tiles on the floor echo to slip slapping of feet
Polo goal posts hanging precariously overhead
A wooden platform for the brave high divers
On the way out penny Brylcream for your hair

Above: Blue shimmering water of Garston Baths at a school gala.

Slipper Baths

To the slipper baths on a Saturday morning
With steaming hot water soft towels and soap
A tiled room with an extra large white glazed bath
Filled to the top sometimes shared with brother
Polished brass taps reflect light from skylights
And a hard wooden bench completed the furniture

Above: The Swan (The Duck) in Garston.

Garston Village Centre

The Village full of banks - shops and public houses
Plenty of pubs and shops to choose from in Garston
The Queens – The Mona – The Mariners and The George
The Dealers – The Swan and the Grand Garston Hotel
Greenalls and Tetleys and Higsons and bass beer
Best bitter and mild and foaming black Guinness
Stated the neat painted signs outside the hotels
Shops pulled down their canvas awnings for shade
On the corner of Speke Road Irwins the grocers
Woolworths had a big store selling everything
We eventually got a television at Radio Rentals
Williams sold new bikes, Elliots sold newspapers
All the shops you needed were in Garston Village
And also banks and the Co-op and the undertaker
Yearly we went to Evans to the Christmas grotto

Above: The Empire Cinema - a magical place.

The Hospital and Cinema

Also up the Village the Empire Cinema or flea pit
The magic silver screen especially Saturday Matinee
With Flash Gordon or The Three Stooges or Zorro
The top of the Village had the Lyceum Picture House
On top of Kettle Nook stood the Alfred Jones Hospital
Garston's pride and joy a place I was grateful for
When a firework went down my boots and exploded
I was pushed in a pram with my foot severely burnt
Once I also split my head open they stitched it up
I walked or was pushed up the hill often to the A & E

Above: Garston Hospital.

Church Sundays

Sundays up early and dressed in our best clothes
Then off to church to worship sing and to pray
At the bottom of our street the Welsh Bethel
In Banks Road Holy Trinity for Roman Catholics
St Michael's C.E. the oldest church in Garston
Based in King Street the Victoria Jubilee Institute
Irish Catholics Welsh Methodists English C.E.
A melting pot under the bridge of all faiths
All working – living – praying together in peace
Sunday a quiet day of rest and roast dinners
The aroma of roasting potatoes filled the air
Family sit down say grace then enjoy a banquet
Streets all quiet no traffic or shops were open

Above: The Welsh Bethel Mission at the bottom of Derby Street.

Garston Shore and Airport

Spent many happy days playing up Garston shore
The shore running alongside the River Mersey
The river rushing in and out washing the beach
Some days so stormy it crashed against the wall
The wall protected the field where we had a picnic
Grasshoppers in the long grass with legs clicking
Butterflies – red admirals and peacocks fluttering
Small blues-commas – meadow browns – cabbage white
In the spring skylarks singing and flying so high
The Airport had long runways alongside the river
Rural peace was shattered by low flying aircraft

Above: The airport with Holy Trinity and Church and Gasworks.

Rabbits and hares went scattering into safe cover
Pheasants flew up so suddenly when peace disturbed
Partridge flew very low and fast when startled
Lapwings nested on the hard ground precariously
Seagulls screamed while sparrow hawk eyed prey
We left behind the hustle and bustle of our streets
A haven of rural tranquillity from our busy lives
A couple of miles of farmer's fields and still ponds
Fields of new potatoes – cabbages – carrots and peas

In hot summers a heat haze rose up from the river
The fields shimmered in the high burning sunshine
Tiny insects buzzed and the hedgerow birds sang
Blackbirds – blue tits – finches and willow warblers
Overhead a kestrel hovered hunting its prey
Weasels and stoats slink in the dark undergrowth
Deep ponds in the fields where we swam and fished
Sometimes the farmer chased us with his shotgun
A boat club for leisure craft and Sunday sailors
Dinghies with their sails flapping in the breeze
Motor boats roaring as they bounce on the waves
A brick built jetty stretched out to the low tide
Past the mud flats as far as the soft sand banks

Above: Garston shore with breaker's yard and fishing boats in the background.

The Breakers Yard and Fishing Boats

Down by the Docks the ship breakers yard
Where once there was a pebbled sandy beach
Now brown slimy mud lay oozing black oil
The mud baked white and cracked in the sun
Ships lay beached with their backs broken
Huge hulks, which once sailed the seven seas
Soon to be reduced to rusting iron skeletons
Once fishing boats sailed from Garston shore
There was still a remnant of the fishing fleet
We watched as they sailed slowly out to sea
At low tide they beached laid on their sides
Their anchors thrown in the mud made a slap
We walked out to them, through muddy water
The boats were painted colours of the rainbow
They had a bridge – port holes – sails and a mast
A few still used their sails most now had motors
Children looked under rocks hunting for crabs
Glass was now a danger from the bottle works
Oil and glass polluting the once pristine beach

Above: The Ship Breakers Yard, Garston.

The Allotments

A trickling brook ran down to the shoreline
On one side the allotments the other industry
Men tended their allotments digging the ground
Greenhouses – sheds – drills of potatoes and carrots
Old tin baths and cisterns storing cold water
A single tap to quench the thirst if parched dry
Hosepipes attached to the tap always leaked
Men and women pushing their wooden trolleys
With their tools brought from the nearby streets
Sturdy built sheds clad with tarred roofing felt
One gardener kept clucking chickens in a hen house
Another man had a pigeon loft next to his old shed

*Above: My first visit to the first field on
Garston shore, allotments behind.*

Street Names

Garston streets with very grand sounding names
Named after writers – politicians – cathedrals – ships
York St. Brunswick St. Chesterton St. Durham St.
Canterbury St. Lincoln St – all cathedral names
All parallel then criss-crossing other streets
Lyon St - Ashton St - Priory St and Window Lane.
Crossing over Window Lane the ship named streets

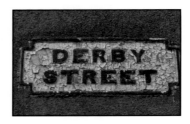

Lucania St – Campania St – Eutria St – Umbria St
Ultonia St – where my mother's family all lived
Vulcan St first built for the Tannery workers
Saunby St which was bombed out in the last war
Our own street Derby St was next to Stanley St
Some streets were named after famous writers
Shakespeare St – Byron St most now have gone
King St – Locke St – Otway St – Thomas St
In King Street the men played pitch and toss
We kept aye-aye out for the local policemen
Sometimes the men would give us a few pennies
Sinclair St – Dale St – Shand St – Leeming St
All knocked down during the slum clearances
We had three little parks around the streets
We had a front door and back door no garden
The front door opened direct into the street
The back door led to alleys known as jiggers
All with nicknames the figure h or enny-ogs
Warrens of escape and for chasing the girls
Bins set in the back wall often went on fire
As did chimneys shrouding the street in smoke

Left: One of the little parks – this one Canterbury Street.
Above: The Top Park, Banks Road – the Hilda Mason
Nursery in the background.

The Top Park - Banks Road

We walked to the park for fresh air and play
An oasis of green amongst the brick streets
It had bowling greens a field and playground
A wooden pavilion with toilets and benches
The bowling greens were perfectly manicured
With stripes of green as smooth as a carpet
Perfect edges cut and gulleys for lost bowls
Surrounded on all sides with wooden benches
A beautiful sight under a clear summer sky
People sit and dream and while away the day
Majestic trees and evergreen shrubs all around
The sweet singing of song birds fills the park
The flower beds with roses of many colours
Their sweet scents wafting around the green
Multi-coloured flowers set in perfect patterns
Busy lizzies – geraniums – lobelia and nemesia
Butterflies fluttering under the orb of the sun
Red admirals – painted ladies and cabbage white
Landing to feast on the sweet nectar of flowers
The restive sound of spectators softly whispering
Occasionally shouting out instruction or laughing
Or listening to the sharp crack of bowls colliding

128

The Bowlers

They had short sleeves and wore white caps
Soft shoes worn to protect the green swathe
The green keeper watched from the pavilion
Where bowls were stored and kettle boiled
Pensioners sat and contemplated long lives
Remembering happy days and years gone by
Men aged seven score and ten dream dreams

*Above: Banks Road Park – bowling greens over the
hedge and trees.*

The Playgrounds

Over the tall trees and thick green hedges
Stood the concrete and tarmac playground
Children played running skipping and climbing
Shrill screams and laughing pierce the still air
Children sit on swings and climb monkey ladders

Above: The Top Park with Banks Road School.

And speed down the shiny stainless steel slides
Whirled around the maypole on clanging chains
We felt dizzy spinning around on the roundabout
Accidents often happened and kids ran home crying
Swings creaked the chains and bolts needed oiling
The park keeper sat in a green painted wooden hut
He chased the children home who were too naughty
Outside his hut was a faucet tap with ice cold water
On a hot summers day nothing ever tasted sweeter
As well as the playground and two bowling greens
A lush green field for football in the cold winter
And cricket was a favourite in hot dry summers

The field was surrounded by rusty iron railings
And trees to climb and collect hairy caterpillars
Often in the winter icy and covered by deep snow
In the summer grass wore out and baked rock hard
In the corner a nursery for babies and toddlers
The babies played outside happily in the sunshine
A colourful scene of toys, trikes and rubber balls
Nurses supervised the toddlers and sat in the sun
As we teased them they laughed back at us daft lads
Some times we were taken to a bigger park miles away
So it seemed to us this park was called Garston Park
It also had a playground and bowling greens and field
But best of all surrounded by a fence it had a theatre
We sat on fold up chairs and watched magical shows
Our school teams also played matches at Garston Park
There was a wooden changing room freezing in winter
I remember prefab housing there as well as allotments

Above: Prefab on Garston Park.

Library

I ventured to the library with eager anticipation
A very small library at the top of Winfield Road
The main library in Garston Bowden Road
Entering you were surrounded by shelves of books
A distinct smell of wax polish and musty old books
You could travel the whole world in your mind
By opening the creased pages of much used books
I read Treasure Island with mounting excitement
Devoured Robinson Crusoe and King Solomon's Mines
Read about sporting heroes making centuries at Lords
And dreamed of scoring great goals in cup finals
My mind transported to Anfield or Goodison Park
Or to Wembley or to the summit of Mount Everest

Above: Garston Library, Bowden Road.
A Carnegie Library.

Window Lane

I would buy Football Monthly Magazine and papers
From Parkers the newspaper shop in Window Lane
No need to go to town or up to Garston Village
You could buy anything you wanted in the Lane
The Gasworks at the top Bottle Works the bottom

Left: 96 Window Lane in 1947
Above: A view of Window Lane showing
the Canterbury (1989).

In between shops, pubs, clubs, houses and factories
Fruit and veg shops, sweet shops and fish and chip shops
Potatoes, carrots, small turnip from the greengrocers
Penny sweets, cinder toffee, toffee apples, ice cream
Stick lice, gobstoppers, sherbet from the sweetshop
Six of chips and best fish or meat pies from the chippy
And can I have the crispy batter bits from the fish
And don't forget plenty of salt and vinegar on top
Hanging on pegs in the newsagents were magazines
You could buy Daily Mirror, The Beano and The Dandy
Ted's barber shop gave you a haircut and penny sweets
A dry cleaners where I took my dad's best Sunday suit
Ardens clothes shop for trousers and plastic shoes

The fish shop for smoked kippers or best yellow fish
Fenelon's butchers for chops or mince for lob scouse
Haberdashery for wood knitting needles or cotton
Dr Goffman and Dr Franklin had a surgery for the sick
Pubs on corners The Rag The Canterbury The Clarence
Windows with signs like snug, bar, parlour, smoke room
A sweet odour of stale beer in the air as you passed
As children we stood in the doorways and looked in
At the men drinking beer talking and laughing loud
It looked inviting colourful and felt snug warm
The clinking of glasses and the wonderful smells
At night the pubs lit up the dark shadows outside
We climbed up on windows and furtively looked in
And tried to watch the television high up on the wall
From the darkness outside the pub interiors sparkled

Above: Window Lane, with fish shop on right, and the Canterbury on the left.

Working Men's Clubs

There were working men's clubs behind closed doors
The Woodcutters started by men from the Bobbin Works
The Woodcutters also had its own Novelty Band
Men dressed up playing kazoos and squeeze boxes
Banjos, tin whistles and the booming big bass drum
The kids of Garston marching happily behind them
Laughing at the men dressed up as big busty women
And sailors and bowler hatted gents and cowboys
They played anywhere for charity and a few pints

Above: The Original Woodcutters Band.

The Blue Union Dockers Club was above a shop
The club built by the stevedores of the new union
Proud to be blue union opposed to the white union
In later years the blue men built a brand new club
Built two storeys high where once we lit bonfires

Window lane had three social clubs and four pubs
One club was behind the shops up the concrete steps
Known as Meredies Snooker Club for men only
As children we were chased if we sneaked upstairs
Downstairs in the yard were stored empty bottles
Some bottles had dregs of beer left in the bottom
We sometimes took a swig before getting chased

Above: A novelty band - a Garston tradition.

Festivals of the year

Easter

The yearly calendar punctuated by age old festivals
Signs of spring starting with yellow daffodils
We prepared for Easter the main Christian festival
With Ash Wednesday we had ashes put on our heads
We would also give something up for Lenten Time
Before Lent we had a feast on Pancake Tuesday
A treat and good fun as sizzling pancakes flew
Tossed in the air flipping to the uncooked side
Jam and sugar – lemon juice all spread on pancakes
Good Fridays no meat and the streets very quiet
No shops were open or pubs and not many worked
The streets were deserted and quietly reverential
Easter Sunday all the streets came back to life
We all wore our best clothes and went to church
The church resplendent with flowers and candles
White was the favourite colour for this happy day
To celebrate we all received a chocolate Easter egg

Above: Family gathering for a christening.

Duck Apple Night

Halloween in autumn so innocent then no tricks
We had duck apple night all and got soaking wet
Apples floated in a bowl you tried to bite into them
Small mouths big apples hard to do without hands
Apples were hung on string from the clothes maiden
Bouncing around as you tried to bite into the flesh
After the games we peeled the apples for good luck
A threepenny bit was also hidden for happy times

Bonfire Night

The Bank was an empty piece of ground in the Lane
Here we played and on November 5th built bonfires
Wood and rubbish collected from all over Garston
Up and down the entries with trolley full of junk
Of wood, old furniture, carpets, lino and mattresses
We ended up rotten and, full of cuts and flea bites
We piled the lot up into a shape of an Indian wigwam
With Guy Fawkes sat on the top ready to set alight
Different streets had their own wigwam bonfires
There was intense rivalry to see who had the best
Raids where carried out and bonfire wood stolen
York Street gang had a bonfire between the houses
The occupants of the houses must have got roasted
As the bonfire flames soared into the dark night sky
The walls of the houses glowed with the flames heat
Fire engines would arrive to dampen down the bonfire
Fireworks banged, whizzed, whooshed and spluttered
Roman candles, rockets, Catherine wheels and bangers

Sparklers held in the hand starred the dark night
Ripraps exploded and jumped around like mad dogs
The night air was thick with smoke and choking smog
Smelling of damp burning for the rest of the week
Clothes singed with a woody smell and dying embers
Accidents happened splinters, cut hands, burned skin

Christmas Time

Christmas started in school with the story of
The Baby, the star, the stable, Mary and Joseph
The Three Kings, Angels and watching Shepherds
It always snowed the star always shone bright
The baby born in the stable was the world's Saviour
Three Kings from afar brought gifts to the new baby
They brought gifts of Gold, Frankincense and Myrrh
But we were all happy because it meant Christmas
We would get gifts if we were good boys and girls
In school we made decorations and a snow frieze
Sticky strips of paper made chain decorations
We put pennies into an envelope for the blind
And marked x in the boxes until it was full up
Days seemed to take forever before Christmas
Excitement mounted as Christmas Eve neared
Would we get the new bike or be disappointed
Would Father Christmas fit down our chimney
We left him a mince pie and for Rudolph a carrot
Kids would go rooting hoping to find presents
The shops all looked bright with flashing lights
And festooned with silver and gold decorations
As we waited we enjoyed the elves and reindeers

We went to see Father Christmas in his grotto
Then sat on his knee smelling his beery breath
It always seemed to snow or was I dreaming
We made giant snowballs and long icy slides
We would cry with the pain as cold hands froze
Eyes watering, ears red burning, feet wet cold
Would throw snowballs and make big snowmen
And clear snow from paths for a few pennies

Above: Christmas Celebrations Banks Road Nursery.

Got to be early to bed on Christmas Eve night
Woke up too early sneaked down stairs quietly
Opened the door to a sparkling Aladdin's cave
Little piles of presents for all the children
Woolly stockings hung up on the mantelpiece
Bulging with tangerines walnuts or sweets
Nothing for naughty children so they told us
We sat in the cold shivering eating chocolate
Parents get up bleary eyed to light a warm fire
Crumpled paper orange boxes coal it all burnt

A shovel covered with the *Echo* helped the draught
The newspaper turned brown then burst into flame
Christmas wrapping paper all went into the blaze
Soon all presents were unwrapped and played with
Books to read also paint boxes and selection boxes
Blow football always our Christmas favourite
Compendium of games, Snakes and Ladders, Ludo
Fire engines, dinky cars, science sets, rubber rings
To throw on numbered hooks with funny faces
Colouring in books with crayons or pencil boxes
Squeaky chalk, blackboards and cowboy six guns
Football boots, football kits and plastic balls
All boys in our house, no prams or dolls' houses
Soon felt sick with stuffing ourselves with sweets
But had to get dressed in our new best clothes
To go to church and see the lit up candled crib
The church pews were packed on this special day
Mum stayed at home to prepare Christmas dinner
The aromas in our house were so mouth watering
Don't eat anymore sweets it will spoil your dinner
We all sat around the table and made merry eating
The lovely turkey with trimmings and Christmas pud
After a happy Christmas the New Year blew in
The ships on the river blew their horns at midnight
Neighbours in the street wished Happy New Year
We blew horns and rattled pan lids and danced.
A dark haired stranger had to be the first footer
And bring with him for luck salt and a piece of coal

Left: Ship and Tug in the Docks.
They would blow their
horns at New Year.

Days Out

The summer holidays lasting forever it seemed
Father took us out for magical trips locally
No foreign holiday or weeks away from home
He took us by motorbike and sidecar at first
Then he bought a magnificent Wolsley police car
With mahogany dashboard and leather seats
The smell of polish and leather was beautiful
The outside was black with shining silver chrome
A Wolsley badge – runner boards and arm signals
We felt like royalty with leather holding straps

Above: A trip out to Sefton Park in the Wolsley.

But for us days out to Seaforth or New Brighton
We loved to sail on the ferry across the Mersey
Watching the Tower and landing stage appear
We raced off as soon as the drawbridge dropped

There was plenty to do at New Brighton such as
Fun fairs, Punch and Judy and games on the beach
Playing in rock pools and eating tasty ice cream
The Pierhead was another favourite destination
With its landing stage - Liver Birds and big river
We would punch our names on strips of tin plate
Preachers would debate with the crowd we listened
Buses terminated here from all ends of the city
As a young boy I rode on the Overhead Railway
Also on electric trams all now retired long gone

Above: A trip out in the motorbike and sidecar – here at the Pierhead.

Seaforth Sands

A drive along the scenic dock road to Crosby Beach
We pitched a tent among the miles of grassy sand dunes
Playing games whirling somersaults in the soft sand
We drank lemonade and eat sandwiches full of grit
Explored the flotsam and jetsam littering the beach
We collected sea shells – seaweed and smooth pebbles
We played in warm salt lakes left behind by the sea
Looked to distant horizons stretching out for miles
We raced along wave rutted sand out to the blue sea
I built sandcastles which stood until tide came in
Skin went red then peeled in the days before suncream
The days seemed so long stretching ahead forever

Above and Left: Sand dunes - Seaforth Sands.

Sefton Park

Days at Sefton Park a lake filled green oasis
A glass house full with exotic palm trees
Surrounded by statues of historic famous people
No need to go abroad when in the glass house
Steaming hot with benches and spiral staircase

Above: Sefton Park Palm House.

A boat lake with rowing boats and motor boats
Dad rowing the boat muscles rippling in the sun
Pirates on the ocean waves rocking with the swell
Motor boats chugging the bows making waves
The rowing boats glided along with oars slapping
Ducks and swans eating bread and flying away
Full flower beds, stepping stones and fairy bridge
We never missed a visit to the always busy aviary

Birds from all over the world including peacocks
And mynah birds - budgies and cheeky sparrows
On the lake we took turns to sail the model boat
Football on the field then ate ham paste sandwiches
We drank Tizer and ate creamy ice cream on hot days
Falling asleep on the way home happy and contented

Below: Model ship sailing at Sefton Park.

The Iron Bridge

I went exploring with friends to the outlying district
Up the cinder path between the Gas Works and Matchies
To Speke Road Gardens or as we called them the Tennies
The Tennies three storeys high with landings and squares
One of the squares had an air raid shelter to shelter in
Not far from the tenements was the railway iron bridge
Over the bridge there were meadows – ponds and hedgerows
We made wooden rafts and sailed on the brackish ponds
The rafts were precarious sometimes we nearly capsized
We took a lot of risks - many times we jumped in and swam
In the summer we watched for the blackberries to ripen
We would search them out among the thorny brambles
Our mouths and fingers bled with the juice of blackberries
A taste never to be forgotten nothing ever tasted sweeter
Then we made our way home back down the cinderpath

Speke Rd Tenements, Garston

Above: The Speke Road Tenements, Garston.

Speke Hall

Another magical place for adventures was Speke Hall
Standing between the airport and the farmer's field
A long trek for us to reach the black and white house
Speke Hall to us a haunted house of ghosts and witches
Complete with dark woods a deep moat and stone bridges
We reached the house through a dense wooded valley
This we called the gulley across which we had a swing
A rope hanging from the trees we hung on like Tarzan
A small stream meandered down to the pebbled shore
Legend warned us of ginny green teeth in the ponds
Waiting to grab us if we toppled in the brackish water
We built dens in the woods among the thick bracken
They were long days of thirst and pangs of hunger
Our supplies of bottled water and butties soon went
The sun would be going down as we wearily went home

Above: The magnificent Speke Hall, where we played in the woods.

The Market

Garston market open Tuesdays and Fridays every week
Stood behind high walls and had two sloping entrances
It had market stalls out of doors and many under cover
Loud traders shouted out marketing their many wares
There was a lot of chatty banter and hustle and bustle
Wafting around in the aromatic air many delicious smells
Meat pies and fresh fish and jam-filled cakes and sweets
After school I would go to the market to do some work
I would help on the stalls or to pack up when finished
I could earn a few pennies or get some cakes or sweets
The market was very colourful and full of characters
The boast was everything was a bargain at the market
And anything you wanted or needed the market sold it
Why go to town the cry when we sell everything cheaper
Buy a suit or a gold watch or cutlery even balls of wool
Or rolls of carpet or pairs of shoes or second hand books
Cuts of meat or reels of cotton even crunchy cinder toffee
Some lonely people went just to meet friends or strangers

Above: The new Garston Market.

Street Dreams

Street Smells

Foggy nights streets disappear under a silent shroud
Haunting fog horns sound warnings on the dark river
A melancholy sound which soothed me to deep sleep
Dreaming of sights and sounds and smells of the street
The smell of the gas works on the still morning air
And the smell of Garston Tannery on very hot days
The smell of road tar bubbling in the hot midday sun
The lovely smell of roast dinners wafting in the air
And the smell of clean rain from heavy black clouds
And the smell from the dust as the rain disturbs it
The smell of my mum's freshly baked bread and cakes
The soap powder smell of the back kitchen on wash days
And the smell of soap suds as front steps are swilled
And the smell of whitening used to blanco the steps
The smell of brasso on the polished door knockers
The smell of chimneys as they spark and go on fire
And the smell of thick smog as the sky is blotted out
The smell of fresh fish seeping from the fishmongers
And the sharp smell of the fruit and vegetable shop
And the bloody smell from the butcher's cuts of meat
The acrid sour smell from the doorways of the pubs

Below: Front and back yard of Derby Street.

Street Sounds

Sounds of the day would also ring in my ears as I slept
The sound of rain storms battering on our windows
The sounds of thunder and lightning cracking the sky
The sound of footsteps crunching in new fallen snow
And the sound of ice cracking in the freezing cold air
The sound of a hard bristled brush sweeping the yard
The sound of fire sparks cracking out of sooty chimneys
The sound of children playing and laughing in the street
And the sound of horses hooves sparking on the cobbles
The sound of the milk bottles shaking in their wire crates
The sound of trains rattling on their iron railway track
The sound of planes taking off and droning overhead
And the sound of ships' fog horns blowing on the river
The sound of buzzers and klaxons from the factories
The sound of neighbours laughing and talking loudly
The sound of the rag and bone man shouting any old rags
The paper seller shouted every night for sale echo-echo
The call of my mother when it was time to come in at dusk

Below Left: Mum on front step chatting.
Below Right: My hair as white as the whitewashed yard.

Above: Local scouts marching in Canterbury Street.

Streets Sights

Sometimes I dream of sights from the old terrace street
The sight of the eastern sun rising over the gas tanks
The sight of the milkman's horse pulling his milk float
And the sight of a leather backed man delivering coal
The sight of a film of oil floating on street puddles
The sight of a rainbow after a sudden wet sun shower
And the sight of rain rushing down the street grids
The sight of snow floating down to blanket the street
The sight of clouds making strange shapes in the sky
The sight of gypsies as they sold trinkets door to door
And the sight of the insurance man on his wobbly bike
And the sight of the knife grinder as the sparks flew
The sight of the bright uniforms of the Salvation Army
The sight of the window cleaner balancing on his ladder
The sight of dust motes floating in the sunny living room
And the sight of steam rising from a drying stone pavement
And the sight of racing pigeons as they fly across the sky
The sight of mother's eyes when I came home from school

Acknowledgements

I would like to thank Countyvise in the production of this book, in particular Charles McIntyre - studio designer - who showed infinite patience with my frequent requests. Thanks must also go to my family who watched me disappear for hours on end, up the stairs to my bedroom to work on this project. Garston Historical Society helped in providing many of the photographs for which I am eternally grateful. I also received photographs from the good people of Garston without whom, this project would not have happened.

I left school at fifteen to be a footballer! Later in life I realised I had missed out on education. It was the 'Second chance to learn' course in Liverpool Community College that gave me the skills and confidence to write and produce this, and other books. I would like to thank them, especially my tutor Eileen Kelly and her staff who encouraged their students with their knowledge and enthusiasm.